i

Pint-sized Plays

Volume Four

Notes on copying and performing these plays

We hope you will want to perform some of these Pint-sized Plays, but possession of the book does not convey any rights to the public performance of the scripts, and copying the book, in whole or in part, would constitute a breach of copyright.

Performing the scripts for free

Your purchase of the book entitles you to apply for a free licence to perform most of the plays when no ticket price is charged: if performing for a paying audience the fee is £5.50 per play, per performance.

Copies of the script for the cast

When you have decided which scripts you want to use, email us at info@pintsizedplays.org.uk with the information below to obtain free PDF copies of the scripts that you can print out for the cast. (N.B. the PDF copies are supplied for your organisation alone.)

Planning performances

Include full details of the performances planned and we will invoice you for any royalties due.

Email the following details to obtain PDF copies of the plays and performance licence:

- Your name
- Email
- Organisation name and type
- Titles of scripts required
- Performance dates
- Venue
- Will the audience be paying in any way?

The name(s) of the author(s) must be displayed on all forms of advertising and promotional material including posters, programmes, fliers and websites. For material publicising public performances, the publisher shall be credited in promotional material, using the words *'By arrangement with Pint-sized Plays.'*

Pint-sized Plays

Volume Four

Edited by Derek Webb

A PINT-SIZED PUBLICATION

Published by
Pint-sized Plays
Glan Teilo
Llandilo
Clunderwen
Pembrokeshire

ISBN 978-0-9576837-3-0

Acknowledgements
We thank the authors for permission to reprint the plays in this
volume. Copyright belongs to the authors. For information about
performance rights enquire to info@pintsizedplays.org.uk .

FOREWORD

As artistic director of a regional producing theatre my shelves are piled high with new scripts that I shudder to admit will probably never get performed.

A small percentage of these scripts should in fact NEVER be put in front of an audience because they are poorly written with stilted dialogue, poor exposition on tired subject matter.

A larger percentage are just not quite special enough to raise their heads above the multitude. They are well intentioned with convincing dialogue and an adequate structure but it's hard to find the original spark, the unique voice that will potentially make a magical night in the theatre.

But there's a very large pile that should be produced or at the very least developed further but finance and time just won't allow for them all on our stages with the tens of thousands of pounds it costs to create one full production in a medium sized professional theatre.

And these are voices that should be heard.

And stories that need exploring.

And it saddens me no end that there just aren't enough weeks in the year nor pounds in the bank to bring these stories to life.

Pint–sized Plays is a fabulous antidote to a world which had consigned potentially great playwrights to the bookshelves of artistic directors like me rather than in front of the audiences where their originality can be heard. They are intensely playful and often the brief to be brief has liberated writers and given them a boldness of style that might have been diminished in a "full-length" play. More than anything an anthology such as this exudes the joy of creativity that comes from writers knowing that their work will be performed and not noted to death through 55 drafts, nor sat on a shelf belonging to someone like me... and they are consequently and perhaps paradoxically a delight to read.

With or without a pint.

Gemma Bodinetz

Artistic Director, Liverpool Everyman Theatre

INTRODUCTION

This year, as we publish our fourth volume of scripts, we celebrate a whole decade of Pint-sized Plays and in that time we have seen many, many marvellous plays demonstrating just how much drama or humour you can pack into a piece of theatre lasting just a few short minutes. When I started the competition the aim was twofold: to encourage new writing for the stage and to encourage new audiences for theatre. In our own small way we have certainly achieved that.

From the thousands of entries over the years, I am pleased to say we have discovered many excellent writers and helped to encourage much new talent. We now handle the performing rights of the authors we publish and their work has been seen all over the world, often I'm pleased to say, in non-theatrical spaces.

That was part of the original ethos of Pint-sized Plays. We purposely put on the plays in the actual bar area of pubs, truly taking theatre to the public. In that way, I hope we have introduced the enjoyment of live theatre to many people who would never previously have dreamt of going into an actual theatre.

Finally, I am absolutely delighted that the foreword for this volume of Pint-sized Plays has been written by Gemma Bodinetz, Artistic Director of the Liverpool Everyman and Playhouse theatres – theatres which have done so much to develop new writing and acting talent over the years.

Derek Webb

CASTING

THE PLAYS

Two Woofs For Yes

by Neil Walden

Characters
*PSYCHIC TED – male, an animal psychic at 'Dolittles, the pet
mediums'*
BRENDA – female, wife of a renowned criminal

Synopsis
*Brenda hopes to contact her dead pets in the hope that they have
witnessed where her late husband has concealed the proceeds from a
big robbery*

Setting and Properties
*Set in Ted's office. It will require a couple of pet collars, a spade, a
torch and a cash box.*

The Author
NEIL WALDEN lived in South Wales for years, but now lives just over
the border in Gloucestershire. His plays have been performed in
festivals and competitions throughout the UK. His more recent plays
include one about the actor Robert Newton (performed in Cornwall)
and Harry Houdini (performed in Aberdeen) but he is always delighted
whenever he is part of Pint-sized Plays whose interest in his early
plays gave him so much encouragement.

TED and BRENDA are sitting facing each other

TED: Just begin wherever you feel comfortable.

BRENDA: Well Psychic, where do you start? Sorry do I call you
Psychic?

TED: You can call me Edward or Ted... Psychic Ted is just a
nickname they give me.

BRENDA: I see... Well then, Ted, You need to understand that my
husband was Billy Wilson... He was quite well known a few years
back... Not necessarily for the right reasons. He was in the papers
every day back then. On the run and then later, when they got him, his

trial was called 'Trial of the century'... At least in *(Insert name of local town)* it was. Anyway he's dead now.

TED: Perhaps I should be clear that I am an *animal* medium... My sensitivity is for contacting animals that live on in spirit form. That's why my colleagues and I call the practice Dolittles... We talk to the animals...

BRENDA: Oh I know that.

TED: So I'm not sure that I'll be able to contact your husband.

BRENDA: Good, I don't want to talk to him. I tried that with another medium a while back and he didn't want to know. But, you see, there's something of Billy's that I need to get back... It's really important. With Billy dying in prison by rights it's mine now... I know it must be in the house somewhere... Hidden. Anyway, I was thinking, back then, we had quite a few animals. One of them might have seen something, maybe they remember.

TED: But this would be some years ago?

BRENDA: Well yeah. But the dog and the cat went everywhere with Billy. If he had the floors up or went up in the roof with all that money then they're sure to have seen.

TED: Money you say?

BRENDA: Yeah, loads of it. Jewellery too, apparently... Look I know it's a long shot but I'll pay extra if you can give it a try... You're my last hope... How does it work? *(Getting purse out)* are you paid by the animal?

TED: *(seemingly shocked)* Please... With Dolittles it's not really a question of payment, in fact we find the notion of payment rather vulgar... We see it that we have been given a gift and we simply want to use that gift to help others... Although... *(Produces a cash box and some forms)* In this case it will be £180 an hour plus VAT, no results guaranteed. Just sign the indemnity here and here and provide the deposit of £95.

BRENDA signs and hands over a couple of bank notes. TED puts these in the cash box which he slams shut.

TED: Right... To start have you got anything belonging to the animals with you? It helps in establishing contact.

BRENDA: I've got a collar. *(Hands over dog's collar.)*

TED: (*starts to feel collar*) Good... Yes (*Seems to be getting some form of communication.*) Close your eyes. Already the spirit lights draw closer.

BRENDA: Do they?

TED: Yes, they are here. They grow brighter.

BRENDA: Already?

TED: Yes.

BRENDA: Where?

TED: Everywhere: around us. Embracing us. Yes... Yes... I see him... Your dear doggie. He has gone over to the other side,

BRENDA: The dark side?

TED: Animal heaven. (*Makes a couple of whining noises like a dog.*) Did you hear that?

BRENDA: Well... Yeah.

TED: And listen now... Scratching, did you have a dog that scratched?

BRENDA: All dogs scratch.

TED: I'm getting a bitch. Was your dog a female? (*Starts to make a low growling sound as the dog's spirit enters him.*)

BRENDA: No.

TED: Thought as much. Castrated wasn't he?

BRENDA: Well yes.

TED: (*Changes to higher pitched growling*) You see that has created confusion... Spirit Guide you have done well... Your old pet dog wants to come to you to bring you peace and comfort.

BRENDA: Does he? You make him sound like Mother Teresa, most of the time he used to be a right little bugger.

TED: What was his name?

BRENDA: Ben.

TED: He is coming through stronger. (*Adopting a ridiculous growly voice*) Mummy, Mummy it's me Ben. There is so much that I want to say, to tell you.

BRENDA: Hello Ben... So what have you been up to?

TED: I've met Jesus...

BRENDA: Bloody Hell.

TED: Sometimes he throws my ball for me.

BRENDA: Oh that's nice…

TED: I miss you Mummy.

BRENDA: Right well, never mind all that, I've got a question for you.

TED: Oh right… Fire away.

BRENDA: (*pauses*) You are sure that you're Ben aren't you? It's just that your lisp has gone.

TED: (*half out of trance like state for a moment*) Wait a minute, the dog had a lisp?

BRENDA: Yes. He had an abscess on his lip that made his bark very lispy.

TED: I see…. Ben where's your lisp? (*Back as dog*) Thometimes it is there… But thometimes it goes… Anyway ath I wath thaying….Thith world where we are is tho beautiful.

BRENDA: That's good… Right then Ben before you go and chase your ball with Jesus… I've got this question for you.

TED: Whath that?

BRENDA: You remember Billy?

TED: He went to pwithon didn't he?

BRENDA: That's the one… Do you remember him hiding some things, it was in a big bag… *(TED slow to answer)* Ben are you still there?

TED: (*in his own voice*) Yes he's still there. He's just finding the lisp thing a bit tiring. Anyway he has a message. He understands your question and he is saying 'Have you looked under the carpets?'

BRENDA: Of course I have. He should know that… Bloody obvious place.

TED: (*to the spirits*) Bad boy, Ben… That's rubbish… *(To BRENDA)* He says he will try harder now.

BRENDA: Good.

TED: *(clearly has no further ideas)* What's that?… What's that, Ben? Oh no he's growing fainter.

BRENDA: Is he?

TED: Yes… And he's gone.

BRENDA: And that's it? *(TED nods)* You get paid for that?

TED: I told you there are no guarantees. The spirits can never be commanded.

BRENDA: I don't know about Dolittles, that's more like DoBuggerall. That's all I get for my money?

TED: I suppose I might be able to coax Ben back.

BRENDA: That would be a first. He never ever came back when we called him when he was alive let alone now.

TED: Hang on.

BRENDA: What?

TED: I am getting someone else. You've got some other keepsakes there have you? *(Reaches over and takes a cat collar off BRENDA.)* I'm starting to get a cat... Is that right?

BRENDA: Yes... Lucy...

TED: Meow.... I think Lucy is at the door.

BRENDA: Tell her to use the cat flap then.

TED: She's coming through... Meow... Now don't just jump in and start asking her where Billy hid the loot... Be gentle right. Now did Lucy have a speech impediment?

BRENDA: No.

TED: Good *(Stupid cat voice)* I'm very shy... *(As himself)* Open up the conversation gently... Give her a starter question.

BRENDA: Like University Challenge?

TED: No nothing difficult. Just be gentle and take your time. *(Cat voice)* Mummy it's me... Lucy the cat.

BRENDA: Hello Lucy... You alright?

TED: *(cat voice)* I am pretty well really all things considered... Meow... Can't complain... I'm here with Ben... You got any questions for me then?

BRENDA: No you carry on.

TED: *(out of cat character)* Look, you're going to the other extreme now... Lucy? *(Cat voice)* Yes. *(Own voice)* Do you remember Billy? *(Cat voice)* Yes.

BRENDA: *(can't contain herself)* Where did he hide the money?

TED: Oh look... You've scared her off now. We were just getting somewhere. Did he have any other pets?

BRENDA: It weren't a safari park... I suppose we had a pond.

TED: I don't do fish.

BRENDA: There were some frogs.

TED: Or frogs, I'm not the bloody Muppet show. What else you got with you?

BRENDA: Nothing, that's it. Just a couple of collars.

TED: Whose is that spade?

BRENDA: Oh yes... Forgot about that... It's the horse's. Not his exactly, but we used it around his paddock for shovelling manure and that.

TED: Right... You have washed it haven't you?

BRENDA: Course I have: that was years ago.

TED: Let me feel it. *(Strokes the spade.)* Yes... Thank you spirits... I'm getting a quadruped.

BRENDA: No never had one of them.

TED: He's coming through... *(Splutters)* He's slowly finding his voice, It's just a hoarse whisper at the moment.

BRENDA: I didn't want a horse whisperer.

TED: *(weird voice again)* Ah through at last, here I am.

BRENDA: Doesn't sound much like Flash.

TED: *(as himself)* You heard a bloody horse talk before have you?

BRENDA: No.

TED: Well then.

BRENDA: Sounds like Ben the dog that's all.

TED: It's a *horse.*

BRENDA: Right, well I'll take your word for it I suppose. Here Flash?

TED: What?

BRENDA: Forgive me for cutting to the chase but was anything ever put in your paddock?

TED: Er no.

BRENDA: Right well bugger off then... Next.

TED: Hang on.

BRENDA: What?

TED: I'm sorry Mrs King. I help people find solace after losing their pets... I will not be reduced to playing Old MacDonald's farm for you.

BRENDA: Well I'll have to find someone else to help me, which is a pity as I'd happily give anyone four times the fee... Ten times the fee, if they could help me find Billy's loot.

TED: You would? Right... Well I suppose I could try again... Funny enough I'm getting a message. It's from another dog.

BRENDA: We only had the one dog.

TED: What? Ever?

BRENDA: Yes.

TED: Maybe it's not a kennel then... Maybe it's a hutch....Did you have a rabbit?

BRENDA: God no.

TED: No, not a rabbit... It's like a rabbit only with feathers. Maybe a parrot?

BRENDA: No never had a parrot. We had a tortoise.

TED: Yes that's what I mean... A tortoise.

BRENDA: I forgot all about him. Lionel is that you?

TED: Lionel?

BRENDA: Yes.

TED: Right... Here he comes... *(Tortoise voice)* Hello Brenda.

BRENDA: Hello Lionel. Fancy you turning up. Do you remember living with us?

TED: Yes... Happy days.

BRENDA: Do you remember a robbery?

TED: Let's think... I use to hibernate a lot back then.

BRENDA: Oh yes, you liked a nice long kip... It's definitely him... Lionel I've got a question for you. Where did Billy leave the loot?

TED: Let me think.

7

BRENDA: Come on Lionel you remember, you went everywhere with Billy.

TED: *(dropping tortoise persona)* Just how slow did Billy move?

BRENDA: No you see he put Lionel in the basket of his bike. Sometimes he'd even put him on top of his head and pretend he's wearing a helmet. You'd think Lionel would remember that.

TED: He may have blocked it out. Pets can be sensitive, they are quite capable of blocking out memories if they have been living in an environment of moral turpitude.

BRENDA: *(puzzled)* He weren't a turpitude... Definitely a tortoise. Didn't even like water.

TED: But he was sensitive to crime that's the point.

BRENDA: I suppose he might have been... In fact, come to think of it, he died on the night of the big robbery.

TED: Aha.

BRENDA: It weren't a coincidence though... Billy trod on him when he was carrying in the mailbags... Really upset about it he was, cried like a baby. Billy had a real soft centre. So did Lionel come to that. He was so upset, he even gave him a real funeral... Can you imagine? Dug a big hole for him in the garden... Really *big* and then...

TED: Sorry... Billy dug a big hole?

BRENDA: Yes.

TED: And where was this?

BRENDA: Down at the boundary with next door's place. There was a row of trees. It was just to the left of that... Thought it was a nice spot for Lionel.

TED: I see... Look, Brenda we've used rather a lot of psychic energy one way or another. Perhaps we can take a moment to re-gather our strength.

BRENDA: I'm not paying for this downtime am I?

TED: No... This is on me... Just close your eyes and relax a moment... I should imagine it's rather dark there.

BRENDA: Where? The spirit world?

TED: No your garden... Where he buried the... er tortoise.

BRENDA: I imagine that it would be at this time of night.

TED: Yes… *(Has rummaged around and found a torch which he is now testing by turning on and off)* Now you stay here with the spirit lights and relax and I'll return in just a few moments.

BRENDA: All right then.

TED: Just relax.

TED exits with torch and the spade.

A few seconds pass. BRENDA opens her eyes checks that TED has gone and puts the abandoned cash box into her bag. Seems cheerful for the first time as she exits

THE END

Two Woofs For Yes by Neil Walden

Attack of the Killer Banana Spider!

by John Moorhouse

Characters
JOSH – Nineteen. Student.
SOL – Nineteen. Student.

Setting and Properties
The present day. A room with two dining chairs and a table. There is a fruit bowl on the table.

Author
JOHN MOORHOUSE is a teacher and award-winning playwright based in the UK and Kuwait. His plays have been performed in England, Wales and the Middle East.

JOSH walks in talking to SOL who is upstairs. He is wearing jeans, a hoodie and trainers and carrying a supermarket carrier bag.

JOSH: No, no, It's OK, Sol. You stay where you are. I can manage. You finish your essay or your FIFA tournament or whatever it is you're doing that's so important. I'm fine. I'll go shopping. I'll carry all the stuff home and I'll put it all away. Don't you worry yourself.

He tips a bunch of bananas from the carrier bag into the fruit bowl and reaches for one. He snatches his hand back.

JOSH: Yaaaaaaarrrgh!

He jumps onto a chair.

JOSH: Shit!

SOL wanders in, in bathrobe and slippers, carrying a toothbrush.

SOL: What's up?

JOSH: Fruit bowl! Bananas! Spider!!

SOL: Spider? You big girl.

He looks into the fruit bowl.

SOL: Yaaaarrrgh!

He jumps onto the second chair.

11

SOL: We had a dog smaller than that. It's a monster! Shit.

JOSH: What is it?

SOL: It's a spider!

JOSH: Yes. But what? Tarantula? Black Widow?

SOL: I don't know, do I? *(Pause)* I'm going to have a look.

JOSH: Don't annoy it.

SOL gets down and goes to the table. He looks.

SOL: I think it might be dead.

JOSH gets down and stands behind SOL at the table.

JOSH: Is it? Please, please let it be dead.

SOL: Or it might just be sleeping.

JOSH: Poke it.

SOL: You poke it.

JOSH: I'm not poking it.

SOL: You want it poking – you poke it.

JOSH looks.

JOSH: It's trapped. See? Its leg's stuck between two bananas.

SOL: Oh yeah.

SOL pokes it with his toothbrush. Pause.

BOTH: Yaaaaaaarrrrgh!

They scramble back onto the chairs.

SOL: *(pause)* Not dead then.

They stare at the fruit bowl.

JOSH: What's it doing?

SOL: It's going mad!

JOSH: It's trying to get free.

Pause.

BOTH: Eeyuw!

JOSH: Did it just do what I think it did?

SOL: It did.

JOSH: It did, didn't it?

SOL: It's a beast.

JOSH: Hardcore.

SOL: Yep. You've got to be pretty hardcore to rip your own leg off.

JOSH: Shit.

SOL takes his phone from his pocket.

JOSH: Good thinking. Phone someone – fire brigade, International Rescue.

SOL: Hang on.

JOSH: What?

SOL: I want to find out what it is first. It might be harmless.

JOSH: It just tore its own leg off!

SOL: We don't want to look stupid.

JOSH: We don't want to look dead either.

SOL: Wait.

JOSH: How are you going to identify it anyway?

SOL: I'm googling it.

JOSH: What are you googling? Banana…Spider?

SOL: Yes. Actually. *(Pause)* Here we are.

He shows JOSH the screen.

SOL: That's it, isn't it?

JOSH: I reckon. What is it? Tarantula?

SOL: Sadly, no.

JOSH: What then?

SOL: According to this, it's a Brazilian Wandering Spider.

JOSH: That doesn't sound too bad.

SOL: *(reads)* 'Also known by its Greek name – phoneutria – which translates as…'murderess'.'

JOSH: I take it back.

Silence. SOL reads.

JOSH: What is it?

Silence.

SOL: Shit.

JOSH: What?!

SOL: *(reads)* 'The Brazilian Wandering Spider also known as The Banana Spider...' See? '...is probably the most venomous spider in the world.'

JOSH: Shit.

SOL: *(reads)* 'Its fangs inject a neurotoxin which causes intense pain, loss of muscle control leading to paralysis, breathing problems and death by asphyxiation.' Shit. *(Reads)* 'In men, its bite can cause an erection that lasts for four hours.'

JOSH: *(pause)* Four hours?

SOL: Four hours.

JOSH: *(pause)* A four hour erection followed by death by asphyxiation.

SOL: Sounds like a Conservative MP's dream, doesn't it?

JOSH: *(laughing)* They'd never get the coffin lid down.

SOL: *(laughing)* Ahhh. Stop it.

They force their laughter down. Thoughtful silence.

JOSH: What's it doing now?

SOL leans forward to look. The chair topples and he lands on his knees by the table. He cautiously brings his eyes up level with the fruit bowl. He freezes.

SOL: Yaaaaarrrgh!

He grabs the chair, rights it and springs back up.

JOSH: What? What?!

SOL: It reared up.

JOSH: What do you mean?

SOL: Reared up! Reared up! On its back legs! It reared up! Fangs...

JOSH: Shit.

SOL: Two...massive...fangs. Oh God. And it swayed. From side to side.

JOSH: Swayed?

SOL: Yes! Yes! Swayed! Like this. *(Demonstrates)* It stood on its hind legs and bared its fangs at me and...swayed. And it...it reached out its front legs...well...leg towards me. I feel sick.

JOSH: Then what?

SOL: It ran off.

JOSH: What? Where? Where did it go?

SOL: I don't know, do I?! I was too busy escaping a four-hour erection and a hideously painful death!

Silence.

JOSH: So, it could be anywhere.

SOL: Yes.

JOSH: OK. *(Pause)* We should find it.

SOL: *(awestruck)* It's as big as my hand…

Silence.

JOSH: These…er…fangs…

SOL demonstrates with two fingers.

SOL: Huge.

Silence.

JOSH: It's probably more scared of us than we are of… it.

SOL: Well, in that case, it must be bloody petrified. And that's just what we need, isn't it? A killer spider from Hell that's feeling a bit hysterical!

Silence.

JOSH: We should catch it.

SOL: *(pause)* Google said…

JOSH: Yes?

SOL: It said that… when it bites, it doesn't always use its venom. Sometimes… it just bites.

JOSH: Sorry?

SOL: Only one bite in three is venomous.

JOSH: And this makes me feel better how?

SOL: I'm just saying. The odds – you know?

JOSH: Well, that's a relief. Let's get after it then and hope we're not the unfortunate one-in-three. Ah! There's two of us, so we could both get lucky!

SOL: *(pause)* We've got to do this.

JOSH: Have we?

SOL: Can't stand up here forever.

JOSH: *(pause)* OK. After three; we'll carefully get down, find it and catch it. One…

SOL: Or kill it.

JOSH: Won't that just piss it off?

SOL: How can it be pissed off if it's dead?

JOSH: But if we try to kill it and miss – it'll be pissed off.

SOL: Actually, I would imagine it's pretty pissed off already. I mean, you would be, wouldn't you? One minute you're wandering around Brazil deciding whether to give someone a playful nip or a four hour erection and an agonizing death. And next minute you wake up in a fruit bowl in a student house in Leeds with your leg stuck in a bunch of bananas. Pissed off? Yep. I reckon. *(Pause)* We need a plan.

SOL looks around then gets down from the chair.

SOL: Cover me.

JOSH: Eh?

SOL: Cover me! I'm going to the kitchen.

JOSH gets down. He holds the chair in front of him as SOL backs out of the room. SOL returns

with a magazine, a plastic bucket and a brush. They get back on the chairs.

SOL: Here.

He hands JOSH the brush.

SOL: Right. This is the plan. First we locate the creature then you use the brush to manoeuver it onto the magazine then I slam the bucket over it.

JOSH: OK. Got it. *(Pause)* Just a minute. What if it runs up the handle? Sod that!

SOL: It's only got seven… six… *(checks phone)* seven legs. It's disabled, isn't it? Anyway, the cold will slow it down. It's used to a hot climate.

JOSH: Didn't look very slow to me.

SOL: No, it'll be lethargic.

JOSH: Lethargic? It just ripped its own leg off!

16

SOL: Swap then. I'll have the brush – you have the bucket and mag.

JOSH: We'll stick to Plan A.

SOL: Ready?

JOSH: Ready.

They slowly dismount and search.

JOSH: Where is it?

SOL: Must be here somewhere.

They search.

JOSH: *(whispers)* Sol...Sol.

SOL: What?

JOSH: Shhh! It'll hear you.

SOL: Do they even have ears?

JOSH: Sh. Look.

JOSH is staring at the corner of the room. SOL looks.

SOL: *(quiet)* Right.

He places the magazine on the floor and holds the bucket ready.

SOL: Go on then.

JOSH: I'm doing it!

He slowly pokes the brush handle into the corner.

SOL: Is it moving?

JOSH: Shut up, Sol. *(Pokes)* Yaaaarrrgh!

SOL: What?!

JOSH: It's got hold of the brush!

SOL: Shake it off.

JOSH flails the brush around in the air.

JOSH: Get off! Get off!

SOL: What are you doing?! On the magazine! On the magazine!

JOSH swoops the brush down over the magazine and shakes.

JOSH: Get off!

SOL slams the bucket down. Pause.

JOSH: Did you get it?

SOL: Most of it.

JOSH: What does that mean?

SOL: Well it's got an even number of legs again.

JOSH slumps into a chair.

JOSH: Oh God. I think I've just had a heart attack.

SOL carefully picks up the bucket and magazine.

JOSH: What are you doing?

SOL: Throwing it out.

He approaches the audience.

JOSH: No!!

He stops.

SOL: Why not?

JOSH: It's a Brazilian *Wandering* Spider. What if it decides to *wander* back in?!

SOL: Good point.

He places the bucket and magazine back on the floor.

SOL: So…What now? *(Pause)* I'll call someone.

JOSH: RSPCA?

SOL: Could do. *(Pause)* Wait.

JOSH: Problem?

SOL: What if they think we pulled its legs off, you know, deliberately.

JOSH: Who, in their right minds, would do that?!

SOL: I'll phone them.

He does.

SOL: Hello. Yes. We've caught a spider. No…I'm not taking the…Listen. Hang on! It's venomous. It was in the bananas. Yes, I'm sure. We looked it up…

JOSH: The bucket!

SOL: Shush!

JOSH: It moved!

SOL puts his foot on top of the bucket.

SOL: Sorry about that. It's a Brazilian Wandering Spider. *(Pause)* Yes. That's right. Four hours. What? Why not? Right. Thanks for nothing, pal!

He ends the call.

JOSH: What did they say?

SOL: Phone the police.

He does.

SOL: Police. Yes, it's an emergency. Yes. We bought some bananas and there's a venomous spider in them. Yes, I'm sure. We looked it up on Google. It's a Brazilian Wandering Spider. *(Pause)* That's the one – four hours. Yes. I know. That's what we said. We trapped it under a bucket. Really? Brilliant! Thanks! 62 Claremont Street. OK. Cheers. *(Ends call)* They're on their way. With... 'a team'.

JOSH: Oh thank God.

Silence.

JOSH: Sol?

SOL: Mm?

JOSH: *(pause)* When did you kick the bucket over?

Silence. He looks.

BOTH: Yaaaaaaaarrrrgh!

They run off. The front door slams. Silence. The spider is still in the room.

THE END

Attack of the Killer Banana Spider by John Moorhouse

Guru

by Jonathan Skinner

© Jonathan Skinner 2015

Characters
*KATE – female, 20s, posh, hippyish, "into" herself
GRAHAM – male, 20s, earnest, naïve, a "seeker"*

Synopsis
Newbie Graham attends a spiritual enlightenment course where old-hand Kate endeavours to show him the ropes.

Setting and properties
*The play is set in a hall or auditorium.
A chair – "Guru's chair" – perhaps on a small raised platform. A vase and flowers.*

The Author
JONATHAN SKINNER is a playwright / screenwriter whose work has appeared on the London fringe, throughout the UK and internationally as far and wide as Sydney, Los Angeles, Ireland and Dubai.
www.jonathanskinner.net

Spiritual music – perhaps a twanging sitar. On a small raised platform, an empty chair: Guru's chair.

Near it, KATE sitting cross-legged, eyes closed, meditating. Composed, self-assured, hippyish in a middle-class, sort of way.

GRAHAM wanders in tentatively. Earnest, a seeker, slightly naïve. He stares at KATE, unsure whether to disturb her. He fights the urge to sneeze but…

GRAHAM: A-choo! Sorry! Hay fever. Didn't mean to disturb you.

KATE: *(startled)* It's alright.

GRAHAM: A-choo! Sorry again!

KATE: Bless you.

GRAHAM: Thanks. Um, are you here for the thing?

KATE: The "thing"?

GRAHAM: Yeah, you know. The thing.

KATE: Oh, the *thing!* Yes. Yes, I am.

GRAHAM: Silly isn't it. Can't even bring myself to say what it is.

KATE: I know what you mean. People tend to think it's a bit odd. A bit wacky.

GRAHAM: I even lied to my taxi driver. Told him I was going to a seminar. "Oh yeah?" he said, "What about?". I wanted to tell him. I wanted to say, I'm going to spend a week in the presence of a living guru, a spiritual leader, a master of divine consciousness.

KATE: But you didn't.

GRAHAM: No. I didn't. I mean, it sounds a bit pretentious, doesn't it.

KATE: Most people don't understand. They're not "ready".

GRAHAM: They think it's weird. Or that you're weird.

KATE: Or they think you're part of a cult.

GRAHAM: Yeah, he looked at me as if I was a bit of a cult.

KATE: Well, I'm glad you're here. Did you follow the path?

GRAHAM: The one that leads up from the car park?

KATE: No, the spiritual path. Did it bring you here?

GRAHAM: Oh, *that* path! Yeah, I suppose it did.

KATE: I'm on the path. The path to enlightenment.

GRAHAM: Right. Great. Me too. I hope. First steps and all that.

KATE: He's beautiful.

GRAHAM: Who is?

KATE: Guru.

GRAHAM: Ah. Him.

KATE: Do you love him?

GRAHAM: I… Well… He's alright, yeah. This is my first time actually.

KATE: We all love him very much. He radiates goodness and wellbeing.

GRAHAM: Have you been to these gatherings before then?

KATE: Oh, yes. The energy. The truth. The clarity. It's overwhelming.

KATE starts arranging flowers in a vase.

GRAHAM: I'll prepare to be overwhelmed then.

KATE: Have you read his teachings?

GRAHAM: Some. I got a bit stuck on identity: "Who are you?"

KATE: *(offers her hand)* Sorry. I'm Kate.

GRAHAM: No, I meant. Who is "one"?

KATE: Ah, right. And? Who is "one"?

GRAHAM: I'm Graham.

KATE: Nice to meet you! *(They shake hands awkwardly)* Have you been on the path long?

GRAHAM: Not too long. I needed some answers. And nothing else seems to make any sense.

KATE: Because it doesn't. There is no sense. There is nothing. There is just "being".

GRAHAM: It's not easy just "being" when you live in a bedsit and work for the council drains department. I need some purpose in my life.

KATE: Then you've come to the right place.

GRAHAM: Hope so. I saw the poster at a petrol station. "Spend a week with the divine leader. Discover the ultimate meaning of life." Four hundred quid including meals and accommodation. It was either this or a week on the piss in Ibiza.

KATE: Then you chose well. Money is irrelevant. A mere symbol of the world's lack of love.

GRAHAM: Have you been following him long?

KATE: Five years. I abandoned religion. Cast it away. I realised how it's totally screwed me up. Do you meditate?

GRAHAM: Um, yeah. I mean, I've started. Recently.

KATE: I go into myself five times a day.

GRAHAM: Really? I'm more of a twice-a-day guy myself. Once in the morning, then again in the evening. A bit like brushing my teeth.

KATE: How deep do you go?

GRAHAM: I make sure I do the ones right at the back.

KATE: No, how deep when you meditate? When you sink down into yourself?

GRAHAM: Not too deep so far.

23

KATE: I go all the way.

GRAHAM: Do you?

KATE: Until I've reached the very depths of myself.

GRAHAM: Wow.

KATE: I "find" myself. When I say "myself" I mean my "self" of course. The "self" within me.

GRAHAM: Right. Gotcha. I think.

KATE: I am an empty vessel that needs filling.

GRAHAM: Yeah?

KATE: There's a way in. You just have to find it.

GRAHAM: I'll try.

KATE: Are you doing the extra course on "being"?

GRAHAM: No. It was another eighty quid. "Being" is going to have to wait, I'm afraid. It's not cheap is it, this finding yourself business? I've signed up for Enlightenment though, parts one and two.

KATE: I'm doing Death and Karma. But, in fact, there is no death.

GRAHAM: Why do a course on it then?

KATE: You have much to learn Graham.

GRAHAM: I guess I do. But I have renounced all my worldly goods. Just like he says we should. Have you?

KATE: Some…

GRAHAM: Aren't you supposed to renounce everything?

KATE: The journey is a gradual one. It cannot be rushed. There was a handbag I wanted to keep.

GRAHAM: I renounced my guitar. Sort of.

KATE: That shows inner strength.

GRAHAM: To be honest my neighbours were complaining about the noise. They said my rendition of Yellow Submarine at three in the morning was too much. So I donated my guitar to the charity shop. Then I realised I didn't want to renounce it after all. So I went back to un-renounce it the next day but it cost me twenty quid to buy it back. Was that wrong?

KATE: Guru says we must do as we do. There is no "right" or "wrong". There just "is".

GRAHAM: Hey, there's a few more people here. It's filling up. Not long now.

KATE places the vase of flowers by guru's chair.

KATE: We must be patient.

GRAHAM: Yes, we must.

KATE: Have you been fasting?

GRAHAM: Yeah. For three days. In preparation. Just like he said we should. Three whole days. Have you?

KATE: Nothing but water has passed my lips. It's supposed to clear the mind.

GRAHAM: To make way for the good.

KATE: How have you found it?

GRAHAM: I've been pretty bloody hungry to be honest.

KATE: Me too. I started getting these splitting headaches.

GRAHAM: I came out in spots. All over my arse. Sorry. Too much information.

KATE: I felt so faint. I nearly passed out.

Beat.

GRAHAM: *(blurts out guiltily)* I had a sandwich on the train!

KATE: So did I!

GRAHAM: Egg mayonnaise!

KATE: Cheese and pickle!

They share a coy smile.

GRAHAM: I had to. I was bloody starving!

KATE: I was ravenous! Afterwards, I felt guilty. As if I'd failed him. But there is no failure.

GRAHAM: It's all part of the journey.

KATE: Have you been ejaculating?

GRAHAM: You what?!

KATE: He recommends total abstinence. Well? Have you?

GRAHAM: You mean ... today?

KATE: Abstinence builds character. We must deny ourselves. We must hold back.

GRAHAM: Well, yes, actually. I have been holding back...

KATE: That is good.

GRAHAM: ...mostly. It's like the fasting. It's not easy.

KATE: You didn't ... on the train...?

GRAHAM: No! Certainly not!

KATE: Good. Nothing worthwhile is easy. The journey is long. We must cross the arid desert of our own ignorance. We must persevere and bear the hardship.

GRAHAM: The hardship. Quite.

KATE: Until we reach the gushing oasis of enlightenment.

GRAHAM: It's certainly going to gush.

KATE: Guru says that life itself shall reward us.

GRAHAM: I bloody hope so.

KATE: We must not live in hope.

GRAHAM: No?

KATE: Hope is always tomorrow. We must live in the present. In the now.

GRAHAM: You're right. Yes. The now. It's just that...

KATE: What troubles you Graham?

GRAHAM: I couldn't help noticing that Guru doesn't seem to deny himself anything. For a start he seems to eat well. He's got a bit of a belly on him.

KATE: He must maintain his strength in order to teach us.

GRAHAM: And he has an entourage.

KATE: Naturally.

GRAHAM: An all-female entourage.

KATE: To manage his affairs.

GRAHAM: His affairs. Exactly. While we his followers...

KATE: He wants no followers.

GRAHAM: Alright, while we his paying audience practise abstinence he meanwhile indulges in tantric sex.

KATE: Because he is The Master.

GRAHAM: So it's alright for him?

KATE: He is Guru.

GRAHAM: If you say so. Hey, I've read all about tantric sex. It's supposed to be pretty tasty.

KATE: So the teachings say.

GRAHAM: Fairly hot apparently.

KATE: When practised rightly, the kundalini energy is released from the petals of the flower that is woman and rises up through her.

GRAHAM: Right. So, um, just suppose, in theory, that he wanted to release the kundalini energy from the petals of *your* flower.

KATE: I would not deny The Master my earthly body. It would be a small return for the wisdom he has guided me to.

GRAHAM: Right. Nice one.

KATE: Perhaps you too will become a master one day.

GRAHAM: Hope so!

KATE: Yes, I feel it. There is a presence about you, Graham.

GRAHAM: Cheers!

KATE: You, Graham, shall one day be Guru.

GRAHAM: Graham the Guru! Wonder if it'll happen this week.

KATE: I live only in the present.

GRAHAM: Me too. What's your room number?

KATE: Forty-three.

GRAHAM: I'm in forty-eight. Just along the corridor. We could meditate together if you like?

KATE: Perhaps.

GRAHAM: I'll bring the joss sticks.

KATE: You're kind. Wait!

GRAHAM: What's up?

KATE: I can feel it! The divine love is approaching.

GRAHAM: Really?

KATE: He is close.

GRAHAM: Oh. Him. Hey, yeah, look outside.

KATE: The Master has arrived!

GRAHAM: Nice Mercedes!

KATE: We must not have attachment to worldly things.

GRAHAM: Of course. I was forgetting.

KATE: Are you ready for his presence?

GRAHAM: As ready as I'll ever be.

KATE: Then prepare for the love and the answers that you seek.

GRAHAM: *(trance like)* I am prepared.

They both sit, eyes closed, serene expressions, waiting.

KATE & GRAHAM: *(together)* Ohmmm… Ohmmm…

Spiritual music kicks in again.

THE END

Art – Or Is It?

by Liz Carroll

© Liz Carroll 2015

Characters
MAN visiting art gallery
WOMAN 1,2 and 3 (played by same person with slight change to costume)
VICAR and MALE CLEANER (played by same person)

Synopsis
A man visits an art gallery. His attention is caught by a painting (not seen but viewed towards the audience). A succession of other visitors all see something different in the painting.

Setting and Properties
Can be performed on an empty stage with no props.

Author
LIZ CARROLL has been writing short plays for the stage for some years. Many of these have been performed at Progress Theatre, Reading in their annual Writefest. Liz also acts and directs and this informs much of her writing for the stage. She has recently had two plays published by Lazy Bee scripts.

MAN wanders onto the acting area; it is an art gallery so he stops a couple of times as if looking at paintings on the walls. He looks out to audience stops, looks puzzled. WOMAN 1 enters – stands gazing at the same spot

WOMAN 1: Oh my god! Doesn't that strike at your very core?

MAN: What?

WOMAN 1: Isn't it the most poignant, the most devastating depiction of the human soul in agony?

MAN: Sorry?

WOMAN 1: Don't you share the artist's pain? He has bared his soul to us. He lays his raw agony before us. All those life colours, all that dancing creativity being dragged down into that pit of grey despair.

See how the grey rises up to drag every last vestige of warmth and humanity into the depths of the abyss.

MAN: Umm… it's not…

WOMAN 1: Have you seen the gallery owner? I must, simply must have this piece.

MAN: No, I'm looking for him myself.

WOMAN 1: You're not bidding for it too are you?

MAN: Er – no. I…

WOMAN 1: I must find him now and I must, simply must, get an introduction to the artist. *(She waves her hands around the room.)* How can the same person have painted this other rubbish?

She rushes off; the MAN looks at the painting again tilting his head to one side and shrugging. VICAR enters during this, wanders for a while then comes to the front and gazes at the painting.

VICAR: Praise the Lord.

MAN: What?

VICAR: What joy, what vision, what hope for sinners and utter majesty for believers.

MAN: Sorry?

VICAR: Surely you must see it man. All that joyous colour rising out of the grey pit of despair. Can't you feel the great transformation? Can't you hear the trumpets? Does not your spirit lift as those colours rise shaking off the bonds that shackle us to this earthly realm?

MAN: I don't think…

VICAR: See the grey rising as it tries to drag them back. But the colours free themselves and rise heavenward…

MAN: Well…

VICAR: Surely no-one can remain untouched by all that rapture.

MAN: It isn't…

VICAR: I say Hallelujah! Hallelujah!

MAN: I really don't think…

VICAR: It will inspire my sermons. I must have it. Have you seen the gallery owner? I must get a bid in for this. The church roof will have to wait.

He rushes out almost colliding with WOMAN 2; she wanders looking at the side walls as the MAN again looks at the painting and shrugs. She stops next to him and looks out to the front – she gasps.

WOMAN 2: And I thought erotica was dead.

MAN: Pardon?

WOMAN 2: What passion, what sensuality – surely you can feel it? *(He looks at her and then at the painting.)*

MAN: I'm not sure you...

A MALE CLEANER enters during the next bit, pushing a broom and watching.

WOMAN 2: It oozes sex. It screams sex. Those voluptuous colours twisting and mingling like bodies entwined in passion on that soft erotic bed of grey. It moves with desire. It heaves with lusty animal heat. It surges up and down and up... It make me feel so... so... *(her panting increases)* Oh Oh Oh Oh Ohhh

MAN: Are you alright?

WOMAN 2: Am I alright? Am I alright?

MAN: Er – I don't know

WOMAN 2: *(she clasps his hands)* I have touched the ecstasy. I am alive again: I came in here by chance and a fire has been ignited deep deep down. I am burning with its passion. I must have it.

MAN: What?

WOMAN 2: The painting! This masterpiece! It will hang in my bedroom. Bloomsbury will live again. Excuse me I must...

She rushes out. The MAN returns to contemplate the painting and shakes his head; the CLEANER joins him.

CLEANER: If you ask me it looks like my four year old's drawings.

MAN: Couldn't agree more. But they all saw completely different things.

CLEANER: That's what they call Transference!

MAN: What?

CLEANER: It's Transference mate. Psychology – I do an evening class on Tuesdays. This is classic. They all transfers their own stuff onto the painting see. Mind you, all I can see is a kid's painting. *(He*

31

points to the walls.) Not like this other stuff – now that's worth looking at. Art Appreciation – that's my Wednesday class. These are good.

WOMAN 3 enters talking on a mobile; she wanders

MAN: Thank you. They're mine actually.

CLEANER: Well they're bloody good. Although this one...

MAN: Not mine.

CLEANER: Ahh. So who did...?

MAN: My nephew. My sister had an emergency and I was looking after him. Had to take him to the studio with me. Let him have fun with some paint and a canvas. Must have been taken for framing by mistake when they collected my stuff. I was just off to find Tim the gallery owner. It'll give him a laugh. He always said I should go abstract. *(They start to exit. WOMAN 3 stops in front of painting.)*

CLEANER: How old's your nephew?

MAN: Four. You were spot on.

WOMAN 3: *(into her mobile)* Such raw talent – a genius... best thing in the place! Superb sense of colour placement. This will sell. Suggest we start the bidding at ten thousand.

MAN: Do you fancy a pint or two? I've a feeling I'm about to come into some money.

CLEANER: Financial management: Thursdays. I could help you with your taxes if you like.

THE END

The Golden Years

by Joe Starzyk

Characters

NORMAN — 60+ male

MABEL — 60+ female

Synopsis

*Mabel and Norman have been together so long that they know
everything there is to know about each other.
Or do they?*

Setting

The set is simply two rockers and a small table between them.

The Author

JOE STARZYK has been writing plays for over 30 years. Since studying playwriting in Oxford, England, he took a 27 year break and in the last 7 years has written numerous plays. His works have been performed at theatres all around the country, Europe, Australia and in Mexico. His play, *Wedding Secrets*, was named the winner of the 2012 McLaren Memorial Playwriting Competition in Midland Texas. Joe lives in Brunswick, NY with his wife Mary.

The setting is a front porch. An older man named Norman, and an older woman named Mabel are rocking in rocking chairs. Between the two people is a small table. They are sipping lemonade. Mabel is also eating a cookie, and fanning herself with a hand fan. They stare forward as they talk. She has a flat demeanour.

NORMAN: Been a long time Mabel.

MABEL: Sure has Norman. Almost fifty years.

NORMAN: Yep.

He sips. She sips, and nibbles her cookie.

MABEL: Been through a lot together.

33

NORMAN: Sure have.

MABEL: Seen a lot of things come and go.

NORMAN: A lot of people too.

MABEL: *(nodding)* True. True.

NORMAN: Always been able to talk to each other. Especially about the weather.

MABEL: Could tell each other anything. No secrets.

NORMAN: Yep. Key to a good marriage.

MABEL: That's what they say.

NORMAN: It sure is. It sure is.

He takes another sip. She takes a bite of her cookie.

I guess it's as good a time as any to tell you that I'm leaving you.

MABEL nods. Then she stops rocking, nodding and fanning. She turns her head to look at him for the first time. She remains unfazed.

MABEL: You don't say? Well… when did you decide this?

NORMAN's face shows he's thinking, but he doesn't look at her.

NORMAN: Dunno. This morning I guess.

MABEL: Well… must have been quite an exciting morning.

NORMAN: It had its moments.

MABEL: So what's your plan?

NORMAN: Move out I reckon.

MABEL: Where will you go?

NORMAN: Guess I'll find a place.

MABEL: *(nodding)* Suppose it will be at Agnes Fecke's house?

NORMAN stops rocking, and looks at her.

NORMAN: What? Why did you… I mean how did you… what?

MABEL remains unfazed as she rocks.

MABEL: I've known about the two of you for years.

NORMAN: *(shocked)* You have?

MABEL: Yep.

NORMAN: But you never said anything.

34

MABEL turns her head to look at him.

MABEL: Neither did you.

NORMAN: Of course not. I was sneaking around. You don't tell someone you are sneaking around. Otherwise it isn't sneaking.

MABEL: *(fanning and taking a nibble of her cookie)* Suppose that's true. But... you weren't really sneaking around.

NORMAN: How you figure?

MABEL: I knew about it.

NORMAN: But I was hiding it.

MABEL: Not very well.

NORMAN: There you go with your negativity. Agnes thinks I do plenty of things... well.

MABEL: She would. She has low standards.

NORMAN gets up from his chair.

NORMAN: She does not. She happens to be a very adventurous woman. If you know what I mean.

MABEL: That may be true. But she doesn't set a very high bar.

NORMAN: You're just lashin' out. You never have anything good to say about things I like. Remember old Blue. You were never nice to that dog.

MABEL: *(shaking her head)* Never liked it. Hated it.

NORMAN: You were probably glad when he died.

MABEL: *(shaking her head)* Not really. In fact... I was quite unhappy.

NORMAN: I'll give you credit for that.

MABEL: If that damn dog hadn't eaten half of your mother's dinner that night, she wouldn't have hung on so long.

NORMAN: What are you saying?

MABEL: That the poison in your mother's food would have worked much more quickly, if she didn't feed half her meal to the dog. Boy that was inconvenient.

NORMAN: Are you trying to say... that you... poisoned... my dog?

MABEL: Not on purpose.

NORMAN: I can't believe it. The dog...

MABEL: And your mother.

NORMAN: *(waving off that idea)* Yeah, yeah yeah... but what did the dog ever do?

MABEL: As unintended as it was, it really turned out to be a two birds with one stone outcome.

NORMAN: Well I'm glad I'm leaving.

MABEL shrugs.

MABEL: I guess I am too.

NORMAN: *(getting very worked up)* Oh yeah. Well... I'm... I'm... I'm gonna take all the money. How about that?

MABEL: Too late. I've routinely drawn money from the accounts, and put most of it in an account with just my name on it.

NORMAN: WHAT? You... you... you...

MABEL: Unusually warm tonight isn't it?

NORMAN: Don't talk about the weather to me. It used to be special, but not anymore. I'll never think about the barometric pressure the same way ever again.

MABEL: Suit yourself.

NORMAN: I'm packin' a bag, and leavin'.

MABEL: Check the front hall closet.

NORMAN: *(confused)* For what?

MABEL: I've had a bag packed for you for over a year.

NORMAN: You're... you're...

MABEL: Very considerate... I know. You always wrinkle everything when you pack.

NORMAN: OOOOOOOO!!!!!

NORMAN makes a highly frustrated noise as he marches offstage. MABEL continues to rock and fan. NORMAN returns with the packed bag.

MABEL: Funny you never noticed any clothes missing. Shows how often you change your routine, or your clothes.

NORMAN: Well I'm changing my routine now. So you better have packed my checkered Sunday-go-to-meetin' pants, because I'm going to be taking Agnes out dancing a lot.

MABEL: That would be something to see. Almost wish I hadn't burned them.

NORMAN: You burned them?

MABEL: Yep. They were so ugly, and they were way too roomy in the crotch.

NORMAN: *(insulted)* They were not too roomy. At least Agnes doesn't think so.

MABEL: I told you… low expectations.

NORMAN: We'll see whose expectations are low. See what yours are like when you are sitting here alone every night.

MABEL: Won't be every night. I've had a standing once-a-week appointment with Hank Green for the last four years.

NORMAN: I don't believe it. You are just saying that.

MABEL: You can check with Hank yourself. What do you think went on around here when you went to all those "Grange" meetings.

NORMAN: *(surprised)* You knew that was phony too?

MABEL: You aren't cut out for sneakin' around, Norman.

NORMAN: I'm leaving… now.

NORMAN starts to walk away without the luggage and turns back.

And you know how you hate drinking, well I've been putting whiskey in my lemonade for years.

MABEL: I knew.

NORMAN: No you didn't.

MABEL: Yes I did. And you know how you hate drugs, well the cookies are filled with pot.

NORMAN: Where would you get pot?

MABEL: My dealer.

NORMAN: WHAT? That's it! Goodbye!

He continues to walk away.

MABEL: You'll be back.

NORMAN returns.

NORMAN: *(indignantly)* Yes I will. And this time I am taking this *(indicating suitcase)* with me.

NORMAN starts to exit. MABEL stands and calls after him.

MABEL: Norman… wait!

NORMAN: *(smirking as he returns)* I knew you wouldn't be able to live without me. And I haven't even left. Don't beg me. It won't hel—

MABEL: *(interrupting)* I thought you should know that the reason you've been… ineffective for a while is that I replaced all your Viagra with blue tick tacks.

NORMAN: All of them?

MABEL nods.

NORMAN: They were surprisingly refreshing.

MABEL: And with Agnes… don't be afraid to have a firm hand on her bottom. Not all of it of course, but whatever you can manage.

NORMAN: What… I…

MABEL: On her bottom. She likes a good squeeze, then a firm tap.

NORMAN: How do you know that?

MABEL: I told you she had low expectations, at least for men.

NORMAN: So you and Agnes…

MABEL: *(nodding)* And Efram, when he was still alive. Regular little Manage-A-Threesome.

NORMAN dejectedly walks away.

NORMAN: I don't get… you and… Agnes… Efram… I can't believe…

NORMAN exits.

MABEL: *(calling after him and waving with her fan)* Bye Norman. Bye.

MABEL sits and fans. She looks just like she did in the beginning.

It certainly is unusually warm this evening.

She takes a bite of cookie as the lights fade out.

THE END

Ruby

by Neil Bebber

Characters
HIM – 64, tall
HER – 63, wide

Synopsis
An embittered husband and wife remind each other of the sacrifices they've made to remain married, as they "celebrate" their 40th Wedding Anniversary.

The Author
After his first play won "Script Slam" at the Sherman Theatre 6 years ago, Neil went on to receive Guardian reviews for his plays *Cul De Sac* (Exeter Bikeshed) and *Straight* (Tactile Bosch, Cardiff). He's since written work for National Theatre Wales, Sherman Theatre, The Other Room, Chapter and Dirty Protest, Cardiff, as well as Riverside Studios, Old Vic Tunnels and Almeida Theatre, London.

He's currently developing three new plays: *Wolf's Milk*, *Rabbit*, and *A Burning Fire* (which he wrote whilst recently on attachment at Theatre Clwyd), as well as two new TV series.

His short story, *Meat*, has just been published in the bestselling horror anthology *Twisted 50*. He lives in Cardiff and is represented by Nick Quinn at The Agency in London.

A man and a woman, in their early 60s, sit facing each other across a kitchen table. An opened bottle of champagne sits on the table between them. She's holding two champagne flutes, filled almost to the top. She holds onto one and carefully hands the other to him. He takes it, reluctantly.

HIM: You're not supposed to fill it to the top.

She ignores him.

HER: Together.

HIM: What?

HER: We say it together.

He puts his glass on the table. Some of it spills onto his hand and the table.

HIM: See. What did I tell you?

She looks at him for a moment in silence, as he licks the spilled champagne off his fingers.

HIM: What? What do you want me to say?

HER: Well, it's your choice, obviously. But what I'd like you to say is, "Happy Ruby Anniversary. I love you." Can you do that? And you have to look at me and say it like you mean it. Even if you don't. (*Pause)* Are you listening?

HIM: Yes. I'm listening.

HER: Well? Come on. She said it's important we do more to make things special.

HIM: Who said?

Pause while she looks at him, waiting for a realization.

HIM: Oh, you mean "the counsellor". I've got jackets older than her.

HER: You do want to make it, don't you?

Pause.

HER: Don't you?

HIM: It's not about what I want.

HER: We've come this far. Made a lot of sacrifices. It would be a shame if it was all for nothing. A real shame.

Pause.

HER: You think I haven't fantasised about being a widow?

HIM: What?

HER: Waking up. You cold and dead next to me. All that sympathy and attention from everyone. Shopping for the right black dress, not too Christmas party, but not too frumpy either, to wear as I watched you lowered into the ground.

Pause.

HER: Don't tell me you haven't woken up in the night, watched me sleeping for a bit and then thought about smothering me with a pillow.

HIM: No.

HER: Really?

40

HIM: No. No, I haven't.

HER: Never wished you had the courage to break the door down while I was having a bath, grab my hair and hold my head underwater until I'd stopped thrashing?

HIM: No. Nothing like that.

HER: Remember that year we went to Dover? For our Silver Wedding Anniversary. And you were on the edge of that cliff, looking down. Teetering. Teasing me. And I told you to come away. But all I really wanted to do was push you. Just enough for you to lose your balance, tip beyond the point of no return. So there would be the briefest moment of disbelief, of delusion, where you convinced yourself that you might be OK, which would quickly give way to the realization that you were about to die... That was the look I wanted to see.

HIM: Why didn't you just do it, then?

HER: Because we had dinner booked.

Pause.

HER: Your brains, smashed all over the rocks below.

Pause.

HIM: Why didn't you mention any of this to the counsellor?

HER: Because I didn't want her to think I was a bad person.

Pause.

HIM: I could have had children.

HER: If you'd been with someone else. Yes. Yes you could. You could have been a dad. A granddad, even, by now. They'd have been tall. Like you. Handsome. Maybe even successful.

Pause.

HER: Too late now, though. It's been too late for about twenty years. I suppose there's a point at which it's easier to go on than start again. (*Beat*) China.

HIM: What?

HER: China.

HIM: What about China?

HER: That's twenty years. China Anniversary. Don't know what it would be in China. They probably don't celebrate like we do, anyway.

Yes. Twenty years is China. Make or break. (*Beat*) Seven years. The seven year itch. Seven years is wool. And wool makes you itch, so…

HIM: That's not the reason.

HER: I know that. I was being funny.

HIM: Brilliant. (*Beat*) And what's forty again?

HER: Have you been listening to a word I've said?

Pause.

HER: What do you think it is?

HIM: I don't know.

HER: Have a guess.

HIM: If I get it wrong, you'll just tell me how stupid I am. Tell me how lucky I am to be with you. Tell me how you're the brains and without you…

HER: (*interrupting*) You are lucky.

HIM: Really?

HER: You don't think so?

HIM: Not particularly.

HER: So all that dressing up in my clothes… (*beat*) …that I never mention, in fact, I'm happy to encourage at times, you think any woman would put up with that, do you?

HIM: It's not as if it's a regular thing. Not really.

HER: Well, just so you know, I've never told anyone, not anyone about it.

HIM: You don't know anyone.

HER: I know lots of people.

HIM: Who? Who do you know?

HER: I know the counsellor.

HIM: You don't *know* her. You talk to her, but you don't *know* her.

HER: I could have told her, though. But I respect your need for privacy.

HIM: So you told the counsellor I hit you, instead.

HER: Yes. Yes I did.

HIM: That I hit you regularly.

HER: Yes.

HIM: But I don't.

HER: No. But you could.

HIM: Why?

HER: Well, all men have a breaking point, the potential to lash out.

Pause.

HIM: I had an affair once. With a younger woman. Ten years younger than you. When I was thirty-seven. You might have told me it was a mid-life crisis. Had you known. You never knew, did you?

She doesn't respond.

HIM: No. I didn't think so.

Pause.

HIM: She asked me to leave you. And I nearly did. Because she was perfect, or so I thought. (*Beat*) You were at work. I booked a day off. To pack.

HER: What was her name?

HIM: It doesn't matter now.

HER: Just tell me her name.

HIM: No. I don't want to hear it come out of your mouth. Now let me finish. (*Beat*) I booked a day off. To pack. And I went to her place. And she answered the door, and she'd been crying. She looked so sad. (*Beat*) I'd never seen her looking like that before… Anyway, she invited me in and gave me the biggest hug. She was like that. Warm. Not like you at all. Anyway, eventually she took a step back, looked me in the eye and told me she was scared. She was scared, she said, because she'd found a lump. Horrible word, that. Lump. She'd found a lump in her breast. And so I picked up my case, turned around and walked back towards the door, without saying a word. And as she cried and begged me to stay, I just kept walking, down the hallway, down the drive. Away. And I came home. I unpacked all the things from my case, put it away, then got back in my car and drove round the corner, where I waited until it was home time. And when I got home, you were there. And you had no idea, obviously. You'd bought lilies, and you were arranging them in a vase at the kitchen table. And you'd bought fruit and filled the fruit bowl. Which made the kitchen look unusually colourful. And you kissed me. On the cheek. Without even looking at me. Not into my eyes, anyway.

HER: You seriously need to work on your delivery. I was starting to drift off a bit, towards the end.

Pause.

HER: I was pregnant. Once.

She pauses for his reaction.

HER: Yes, I know. They told us it wasn't possible. Well, it was. Six years in. Sugar. That's six years.

Pause.

HER: What do you think it was? Boy or girl?

HIM: Don't…

HER: It was a boy. And I was lying awake every night. Because I wanted to tell you. Find a way of telling you. I didn't want it. Because it would have come between us. Distracted us from each other. And I waited, right until it was almost too late. Two more days and I'd have had to go to some dodgy backstreet place. I might not have been here now. Anyway, after, you know, after they'd removed it, they asked me if I wanted to see it. Which I don't think they should have. But, anyway, I did. And, like I said, it was a boy. You could clearly see it was a boy. And he already had enormous feet. Just like you.

Pause.

HER: Anyway. Ruby. That's forty. Forty years today. Platinum's seventy years. Just thirty more years. Think we'll make it? I hope so. I really do.

He sits in stunned silence.

HER: Yes. You're right. One year at a time. Silly cow.

She stands, raises her glass of champagne.

HER: Well?

He pauses. Then stands.

HER: Together…

TOGETHER: Happy Ruby Anniversary. *(Pause)* I love you.

They clink glasses, neither making eye contact.

THE END

Serenity Island

by Kay Phillips

© Kay Phillips 2015

Synopsis
A patient at a productivity detoxification facility gets caught committing the ultimate sin: work.

Characters
DOCTOR – any age, dedicated to his work, a bit scary
NURSE – any age, loyal and a bit naïve
KARL – 30s-50s, frazzled workaholic

Setting and properties
Table, two chairs, CD player, tropical drink

Author
KAY PHILLIPS is an award-winning screenwriter and internationally produced playwright. Her stage plays have been performed on five continents, including performances in London, Sydney, Toronto, and Johannesburg. In 2015, her full-length play *The Ladies of Friscitana, Texas* was workshopped with the Modern Day Griot Theatre Company in Brooklyn, NY and her play *She Keeps This Family Together* debuted off-off Broadway with The Gallery Players in NYC.
Upcoming projects include the world premiere of her play *The Unders* in Los Angeles. Kay is a member of the Dramatists Guild of America and lives in Arizona.

DOCTOR, ageless, mad scientist type, and NURSE in a sparsely furnished doctor's office. DOCTOR sits behind his desk when the NURSE enters. As she opens and shuts the door quickly, painful screams are heard. DOCTOR looks up.

DOCTOR: Patient 1508?

NURSE: More of the same, doctor. I just wish there were some way we could help him, but I'm afraid we may be too late.

DOCTOR: He did it to himself, nurse. They all did. Remember, we cannot help those bent on self-sabotage.

NURSE: Self-sabotage? What did you mean? You didn't find—?

DOCTOR nods, throws a smartphone on the desk between them. NURSE gasps

NURSE: You mean he's been—?

DOCTOR: *(overlapping)* That's right. The son of a gun has been *working.*

NURSE: Oh, no!

DOCTOR: Oh yes. Secretly dialing into board meetings, IM'ing clients from off-site. Spreadsheets, pie graphs, you name it. It's disgusting. And it's been going on right under our noses.

The intercom on the doctor's desk buzzes. He pushes the button.

DOCTOR: Send him in.

Seconds later, the door opens and KARL, a 30ish businessman with a crazed, wild look stumbles in. He wears the tatters what used to be a classy suit. The NURSE guides him to the chair in front of the doctor. He sits heavily.

DOCTOR: Ah, Patient 1508. *(Holds up the smartphone.)* Care to explain?

KARL: Where did you get that? Who gave that to you? That's my private property.

DOCTOR: I'm afraid it's now the property of Serenity Island Resort and Spa. Now, Karl – may I call you Karl? I'm going to ask you a simple question: from whom did you receive this?

Pause.

KARL: Nobody. I... I smuggled it in past the concierge.

DOCTOR looks at NURSE, wanting an explanation.

NURSE: But we checked, doctor. We give everyone a thorough search before arriving. It couldn't have been on his person.

DOCTOR: *(to KARL)* Tsk. Tsk. I have to say I'm deeply disappointed in you.

DOCTOR nods to NURSE, she searches through the cabinets, KARL notices.

KARL: Wait, wait! What's she doing, doc? What're you guys gonna do to me?

DOCTOR: Obviously, routine retraining methods have had little effect on you, so—

NURSE pulls out a CD player, KARL looks terrified.

KARL: No! No! I've heard about this. Oh, God, no! Not—

DOCTOR: Oh, yes, Karl. It's the only way.

KARL squirms in his chair as NURSE ties him up. DOCTOR gets up from his seat, calmly looks through the CD collection.

DOCTOR: Don't you see, Karl? You're physically unable to relax. You just can't do it. But, we've got just the thing. Oh, yes. The proverbial "cure all", if you will. Nurse, is the limbo song ready?

NURSE: Yes, doctor.

DOCTOR: Then, cue Harry Belafonte!

KARL: No!

NURSE takes the CD from him, starts to put it in the player.

KARL: *(frantic)* Wait!

NURSE and DOCTOR freeze.

KARL: *(desperate)* I can... I can change. I swear I can! I won't touch the phone. I won't talk about spreadsheets or... or profit margins or...

DOCTOR: PowerPoint?

KARL: No.

DOCTOR: Excel?

KARL: No. I swear on my mother.

Pause.

KARL: What do you say, Doc? Give me a chance!

DOCTOR:

Perhaps, but...

KARL: Put me on twenty-four hour watch. I'll even take solitary confinement.

DOCTOR: "Solitary?"

KARL: Sundeck. I meant, sun deck confinement.

DOCTOR: *(shakes his head)* I wish I could believe you, Karl. Nurse, bring the shuffleboard equipment and a fruity drink. Patient 1508 has forgotten where he is.

NURSE: Yes, Doctor.

She leaves

KARL: I haven't forgotten.

DOCTOR: No? Then, where are you?

KARL mumbles

DOCTOR: I'm sorry, I didn't catch that. Speak up, Karl.

KARL: *(louder)* Vacation.

DOCTOR: That's right. Vacation. And what is our motto here at the Serenity Island Resort and Spa?

KARL: *(recites)* 'Enjoy the sun and surf while making a concerted effort at forgetting the cares of the outside world and merriment".

DOCTOR: *(overlapping)* "Merriment". Exactly. And how many times have you been down to the water's edge, Karl, to make merry?

Silence.

DOCTOR: How many complimentary Fruity Patooties have you enjoyed at happy hour?

Silence.

DOCTOR: You didn't even know we had happy hour, did you?

NURSE returns with the cart with CD player, tropical drink on it. KARL whimpers.

NURSE: Standing by, doctor.

DOCTOR: *(to KARL)* Do you see my dilemma, Karl? Half of me wants to let you off with a stern warning that you cease this business of "business" immediately and the other half—

He thrusts his face just inches from the nervous Karl.

DOCTOR: —just wants to Jimmy Buffett you until it hurts. *(To NURSE)* Strap him in.

KARL struggles uselessly as the NURSE sets him in the chair; she puts a hat on his head, the drink in his hand and turns on the tropical tunes, KARL screams in agony.

KARL: No! God help me!

DOCTOR: *(to NURSE)* Nurse, the volume.

She turns it up. KARL howls.

DOCTOR: We've run out of options, Karl. But we could've avoided all this if you would just tell me where you got this nasty, filthy piece of—

KARL: *(screams)* Andy! It was Andy!

DOCTOR holds up a hand for the NURSE to turn down the music

DOCTOR: Andy Talbert?

KARL nods furiously

KARL: Andy was the one that smuggled it in, not me. I told him I wouldn't tell, but you brought out the Jimmy Buffet and the limbo song and you broke me. My God, you broke me!

KARL collapses, sobbing. DOCTOR motions for the NURSE to pause the music

DOCTOR: Congratulations, Patient 1508. You just bought yourself one more day in paradise. Consider yourself lucky. Nurse, if you please.

The NURSE unstraps him

KARL: What are you gonna to do to Andy?

DOCTOR: Never you mind. I'll take care of Patient 1616. *(Checks his watch.)* You'd better hurry, Karl. We don't want to be late for cabana karaoke, do we?

KARL: No, doctor.

He shuffles out, defeated. Meanwhile, DOCTOR is energized. He snaps on rubber gloves, slips into a white lab coat.

NURSE: Doctor?

DOCTOR: Fetch me Patient 1616, Nurse. And some SPF 15, flip-flops man sized eleven and a pair of lime green arm floaties.

NURSE: Arm floaties? But doctor, it was just a phone.

DOCTOR: *(titillated by his own thoughts)* A conga line. Yes. A conga line with flower leis and coconut drinks and... and... you're still here?

NURSE: *(resigned)* Sorry, doctor.

She leaves. DOCTOR laughs maniacally. Music continues to lights fade.

THE END

Serenity Island by Kay Poiro

Beam Me Up Doctor

by Jaye L Swift

Characters
KEITH – Cafe Owner
VULCAN (male)
DOCTOR (female)

Synopsis
There is a Sci-Fi convention on in town. Geeks, nerds and cosplayers (geeks and nerds who dress up in costumes) are everywhere. Help is at hand when one of the cosplayers ends up lost and stumbles into a cafe.

Setting and Properties
Tables and chairs, coffee cups, welsh cakes, convention poster, mobile phones

The Author
JAYE SWIFT, born in Malawi, but moved to England when she was six, lives in the Vale of Glamorgan. She ran her own photography business for eighteen years before writing for stage and screen. She has had plays short-listed and performed as rehearsed readings by Spread the Word (Sherman Cymru) and Pontardawe Script Slam. Plays produced by Pint-Sized Plays, Mercury Theatre Wales and Fluellen Theatre. A short film script produced by It's My Shout was screened on BBC TV during December 2014. She has also written and produced her first short film set during WW1 called *Letters Home.*

Inside the cafe: tables, chairs, menus, sci-fi posters slapped on walls /sci-fi flyers on tables. KEITH dries a coffee mug, hums aimlessly. In stumbles, from stage left, a VULCAN, who looks disorientated. KEITH gives the VULCAN a once over, snorts.

KEITH: Alright, mate?

The VULCAN is dressed in a poorly fitted 'Mr Spock' Star Trek costume; his black trousers flap hilariously above his ankles, his 'tight fitting' blue t-shirt is quite blousy, his short black wig sits precariously on his head, his pointed ears are huge and obviously fake.

VULCAN: Think I'm lost.

KEITH: Off to the sci-fi con are we?

The VULCAN withdraws a mobile phone from his trouser pocket, stabs at it.

VULCAN: Come in transporter room, do you read?

KEITH guffaws. The VULCAN stares at his mobile, wills it to answer.

A palpable silence.

He glances at KEITH, plonks down at a table, grabs a menu, studies it.

VULCAN: Coffee, please.

KEITH: Intergalactic coffee would that be?

The VULCAN, un-impressed.

VULCAN: Just normal – one shot.

KEITH: As you are.

KEITH sets about making the coffee, one eye glued firmly on the nerd at the table.

The VULCAN fidgets, fiddles with his wig, knocks it askew, straightens it, dislodges his fake ear. It bounces off the table onto the floor.

KEITH, desperate not to laugh, concentrates on making the coffee. The VULCAN retrieves his ear from the floor, reattaches it to his head.

KEITH places the coffee in front of the VULCAN. The VULCAN searches for change to pay, KEITH waves it away.

KEITH: Didn't think you needed money, you know, up there in outer space?

The VULCAN stabs at his mobile again.

VULCAN: Transporter room, come in please.

KEITH perches on another table with mug of tea.

KEITH: Used to like all that final frontier stuff when I was a kid, dressed up too, kind of grown out of it now.

The VULCAN stabs at his mobile.

VULCAN: They can't operate without me. I have the plans.

KEITH: Ah, yes. The plans.

VULCAN: Transporter room? *(Stabs)* Engine room? *(Stabs)* Bridge? *(Stabs)*. Hello? Hello? Anyone there?

KEITH: Looks like no-one's home – maybe they fell through a black hole. *(Laughs)*

VULCAN: Nearest black hole's light years away.

KEITH: Course it is.

The VULCAN sips his coffee.

VULCAN: Got any Welsh cakes?

KEITH chokes on his tea, grins.

KEITH: Coming right up.

He fetches Welsh cakes, plonks them on the table, the VULCAN devours them.

KEITH: Hungry, this space travel lark?

The VULCAN nods, scoffs another cake.

KEITH: So, your friends?

VULCAN: My landing party?

KEITH: Yep, them. Where are they?

VULCAN: *(shrugs)* There was a glitch with the transporter.

KEITH: I could phone a breakdown company.

VULCAN: Breakdown company?

KEITH: For your car.

VULCAN: Who said anything about a car?

KEITH stares at the VULCAN. The VULCAN tries his mobile again.

VULCAN: Come in transporter room.

He looks at KEITH.

VULCAN: Nothing.

A ring tone emits from the VULCAN's mobile.

Ring tone: Warning – warning – it's the wife. Warning – warning.

The VULCAN ignores it.

KEITH: You going to get that?

VULCAN: What?

KEITH: The message.

VULCAN: What message?

KEITH: Oh, you're good – you're very good keeping in character and all that, but mate – just look at yourself.

The VULCAN stares at KEITH.

KEITH: I've seen better costumes in a kiddie's playgroup.

VULCAN: Costumes?

KEITH: Yeah, costumes.

VULCAN: Are you referring to my uniform?

KEITH stares at the VULCAN, then roars with laughter.

KEITH: You geeks crack me up. Aw, this is brilliant. OK, then. What's your mission – other than to get to the convention?

VULCAN: Mission?

KEITH: You know, to boldly go, or in your case – to Wiggy go. *(Laughs at joke.)*

The VULCAN indignant, adjusts his wig, his ear dislodges and plops into his coffee. KEITH roars.

The VULCAN retrieves his ear, wipes it on his t-shirt, re-attaches it to own his ear – backwards.

KEITH: It's on the wrong way.

The VULCAN, confused.

KEITH: Your ear *(laughs)*. You've got to turn it around.

The VULCAN does nothing.

KEITH is in stitches.

KEITH: Seriously mate, want me to order a taxi, get you to the con?

VULCAN: You keep going on about a con.

KEITH: The sci-fi weekend extravaganza – we've had all sorts of aliens through this weekend.

VULCAN: Aliens?

The VULCAN jumps to his feet, unholsters a badly made laser gun made from a shampoo bottle and gaffer tape.

VULCAN: Which aliens?

KEITH stares at the VULCAN, open mouthed.

KEITH: You're nuts.

VULCAN: Been tracking the Dondoodles for weeks.

KEITH: Dondoodles?

VULCAN: Nasty blighters, worse than rats, breed like rabbits, eat shoes.

KEITH, lost for words.

VULCAN: Did they pass this way?

KEITH: You're seriously off your head, mate. It's a sci-fi convention, it ain't real!

VULCAN: If you've seen the Dondoodles, you must tell me. Lives could be at stake.

KEITH: You've got fake ears for Christsakes!

VULCAN: Going to have to warn the local population.

KEITH: You're wearing a wig!

The VULCAN stabs at his mobile.

VULCAN: Transporter room, anyone... be warned... they are here...

KEITH: You've got a fake laser!

VULCAN: I repeat, the Dondoodles are here.

KEITH, exasperated.

From stage left in walks the DOCTOR, her 'Tom Baker' Dr Who costume appalling. The long coat is a brown dressing gown, the multi-coloured scarf is impressively over long, and her hat is a crumpled felt fedora.

KEITH lets out long painful sigh.

KEITH: Ain't you supposed to be a bloke?

DOCTOR: Excuse me?

KEITH: The Doctor is a man.

DOCTOR: I assure you I'm all female.

KEITH: Yeah, bet you are... and you're the real deal no doubt, like Mr Spockett over there.

The DOCTOR glances at the VULCAN.

VULCAN: He's seen the Dondoodles.

The DOCTOR whips around looks KEITH up and down.

DOCTOR: Did you touch them?

KEITH: What?

DOCTOR: The Dondoodles?

KEITH: There are no Dondoodles. You lot are bloody insane!

VULCAN: I beamed down with my party to find them, hunt them down.

DOCTOR: And?

VULCAN: I've lost my party.

KEITH: Lost your bloody marbles more likely.

The DOCTOR whips around to face KEITH.

DOCTOR: You have marbles?

KEITH: What?

DOCTOR: Large ones?

KEITH: What the hell are you on about?

VULCAN: I lost mine, but if this local has some, it will certainly help.

DOCTOR: May we have your marbles, sir?

KEITH, dumbfounded.

DOCTOR: It's the only weapon that will kill them.

VULCAN: My laser will stun them, *(waves gaffer taped shampoo bottle around)* but it's marbles that'll finish them off.

KEITH, catches his breath.

KEITH: Get out, you crazy sons of bitches.

VULCAN: Is that wise, with the Dondoodles out there?

A strangled scream from KEITH.

KEITH: I don't care about your stupid Dondoodles; I want you out of my cafe!

DOCTOR: And the marbles?

KEITH: There are no marbles! There are no Dondoodles! You are not The Doctor! And you are not off the Starship bloody Enterprise!

Stunned silence.

All three look at one another. The VULCAN stabs at his mobile.

VULCAN: If anyone is receiving, please be warned of a Dondoodle sympathiser.

KEITH: Right, that's it! I want you loonies out, right now!

VULCAN: I can't leave.

KEITH: You can, too.

KEITH grabs the VULCAN's arm, dislodges his ear. It falls to the floor. They all stare at it.

DOCTOR: You can come with me.

The DOCTOR scoops up the ear, hands it to the VULCAN, who shoves it in his pocket.

DOCTOR: My transporter is out the back.

KEITH: No it ain't. Come on guys, just go.

DOCTOR: *(to the VULCAN)* if you give me your co-ordinates I can return you to your ship.

KEITH: Out!

VULCAN: That'll be a logical move. I can warn the Galactic Federation that the Dondoodles have invaded earth.

KEITH: Now!

The DOCTOR indicates stage right, the VULCAN heads that way.

KEITH: Not that way. That's the way out. *(Points stage left.)*

DOCTOR: If you'd excuse us.

The DOCTOR pushes past KEITH, the VULCAN follows.

KEITH: I don't think so!

KEITH attempts to block the DOCTOR and the VULCAN; they exit stage right.

KEITH goes to make chase. Stops abruptly. His jaw drops when he hears the unmistakable sound of the Tardis.

The sound fades away.

KEITH smiles, takes out his own mobile phone.

KEITH: Calling all Dondoodles... calling all Dondoodles. It's OK, I've fooled them, they've gone away. Big party in the cafe tonight! Bring your own shoes!

THE END

Beer Window

by Neil Walden

© Neil Walden 2015

Characters
SOPHIE – Female, can be almost any age
BEN – Male. Partner of SOPHIE and so likely to be of a similar age.
He wears a bandage on his bad leg and limps when walking, although
he sits throughout most of the play.

Synopsis
While Ben is confined to his room with a bad leg he has taken up
spying on the neighbours. He is now convinced that he has witnessed
a murderer at work.

Setting and Properties
The play was originally performed in pubs where the binoculars used
were simply upturned beer glasses. If performed elsewhere, ordinary
binoculars can be used. Also need a voice recorder, wig and dress.

The Author
NEIL WALDEN has had his plays performed in various festivals and competitions around the UK. Most recently he has been writing a series of publications for *Bradwell Books* which chronicle true murder stories from various parts of Britain. None of the stories recounted there are as mysterious as the strange case of the *Beer Window…*

The action takes place in Ben's apartment. BEN is frequently staring at, and above, the audience through binoculars as if looking through a window.

BEN: (*looking through binoculars and talking into a voice recorder*) 15.34 hours... Suspect returns to the flat. Puts bag in hall... It is a white plastic bag... It contains... Umbrella... Bag also contains a black leather handbag with silver clasps, that's interesting... This is carried through to kitchen by suspect. (*He tracks the suspect across the windows of the flat.*)

SOPHIE: (*entering and shaking her head*) Caught you... You're doing it again.

BEN: *(instantly switching direction of binoculars)* The largest of the duck-like animals leaves the bird table and returns to the nest.

SOPHIE: You're not fooling anyone.

BEN: I'm bird watching.

SOPHIE: Maybe that's how it started, but I know what you're up to.

BEN: I'm a twitcher, you know I am.

SOPHIE: A curtain twitcher – you're becoming like that guy in the Hitchcock film.

BEN: *The Birds*? Exactly – I'm a keen ornithologist.

SOPHIE: No I mean the one about the peeping Tom.

BEN: Yes well I'm incapacitated aren't I? Trying to adapt to my life-changing injury. The doctor said that it was the biggest muscle tear he'd ever seen.

SOPHIE: No... Biggest *fuss* is what he said. *(Takes off coat and puts down the bag she's been carrying.)* So?

BEN: What?

SOPHIE: Go on then... Anything to report?

BEN: Aha.

SOPHIE: What?

BEN: See. You are interested. Well, I can reveal that the man opposite, the one on the fourth floor...

SOPHIE: Yes?

BEN: He's just come back.

SOPHIE: Is that all? I already know that, he was on the bus with me.

BEN: Was he? I'll make a note of that... *(Jots it down.)* On bus with Sophie... I hope you kept your head down and didn't blow my cover.

SOPHIE: Why would he suspect anything? Isn't talking to people more normal than spying on them?

BEN: I just hope you weren't too obvious.

SOPHIE: No you're safe, I had a newspaper with eyeholes cut in it so he wouldn't suspect anything.

BEN: You spoke with him?

SOPHIE: I just said *hello* when we got off.

BEN: Hang on, let me get this. *(Jots down)* Sophie said Hello.

SOPHIE: We went different ways. He went straight home... As you saw... and I went to pick up something from the shop.

BEN: Let's see... He got in at 15.34. Quite early for him I thought.

SOPHIE: *(seeing BEN's paperwork)* What's that there?... Oh for God's sake... You've got notes of all his movements?

BEN: No... It's a graph... You can do all that in EXCEL really easily.

SOPHIE: You've got a database? That's unbelievable... What are you hoping to find?

BEN: I'll tell you when I find it.

SOPHIE: Look... Ben... I'm worried about you.

BEN: Don't be... What else can I do? Just stuck in the house like this?

SOPHIE: There must be other things.

BEN: Well... Yes. But when I've done those things I pour myself a beer and...

SOPHIE: Spy on the neighbours.

BEN: No... Watch the World go by. It's my *beer window.*

SOPHIE: You need to ask yourself: Is it ethical to watch all the neighbours with binoculars all the time?

BEN: I have... I'm not stupid... I'm aware that it raises important ethical questions about privacy and public interest. I've thought long and hard about it. Really I have...

SOPHIE: Good.

BEN: And, on balance, I think it's for the best. I want people to think of me as keeping an eye out for them. Like Orwell's Big Brother, only more *caring.*

SOPHIE: Sorry Ben, I'm really uncomfortable with this.

BEN: I was uncomfortable too... At first, I know precisely what you mean... But then I got some extra cushions and I was *really* comfortable... Come on pull up a chair... This is great... All human life is here in front of us and it doesn't cost a bean.

SOPHIE: You *will* stop all this when you're leg's better?

BEN: Of course I will.

SOPHIE: I don't know why you couldn't just watch the sport on the TV like everyone else.

BEN: Because this is real life, not a game. Go on... Pour us both a drink and pull up a chair at the beer window. *(For the first time SOPHIE reticently attempts to look out of the window.)* There... See, it's interesting. There's another pair of binoculars for you there.

SOPHIE picks up binoculars and looks.

SOPHIE: Don't think much of his wallpaper.

BEN: See it's addictive. Anyway, look at this. *(He passes her a sheet of paper.)*

SOPHIE: What am I looking at?

BEN: There. *(Pointing at paper)* Your friend on the bus: See, he goes out. The house is empty for an hour, then a woman.... Similar age, blonde, green dress – I assume it's his wife, comes home.

SOPHIE: So?

BEN: With another man.

SOPHIE: And what happens?

BEN: I don't know... Not for a fact... She pulls the curtains... Selfish I call it. Next morning the curtains open and the first man, your friend from the bus, is back in the house... Alone. No sign of the blonde woman. No sign of the second man.

SOPHIE: They probably work different shifts or something. I expect he comes back in the middle of the night.

BEN: No, that's not possible.

SOPHIE: How do you know? Oh God, don't say that you've been sitting up all night?

BEN: I have to… It's the pain of the injury. *(Points at foot.)*

SOPHIE: And that's it is it? You sit up all night and that's all that happens?

BEN: No. There's more... The day before yesterday the blonde woman returns, same green dress... and she's with *another* man.

SOPHIE: The second man again?

BEN: No... A third one... I hadn't seen him before. She goes to the window, she closes it, then she pull the curtains and then…

SOPHIE: Don't tell me... Nothing happens?

BEN: *Exactly, EXACTLY...* But the next morning the first man is back, no sign of his wife and no sign of her latest lover. Don't you think that's odd?

SOPHIE: No... Complicated maybe.

BEN: No it's simple. Treat it as an equation... With X being the unknown quantity. The blonde woman we'll call Y.

SOPHIE: Why?

BEN: Stop it, I'm explaining... And your friend from the bus we'll call Z... Y never meets Z. They *never* meet, they never say goodbye... We know nothing about the mystery woman... Codename 'Y'... All we know is that she shuts the window. That's another thing. Why does she do that? Scared of being burgled? Scared of creepy crawlies?

SOPHIE: Yes, she's probably scared of creepy crawlies coming in. Although that's quite unlikely when you think about it... I mean for a start off you would have to crawl across the road to get over there now that your leg's playing up.

BEN: But don't you think it's odd?

SOPHIE: No, and it's nothing to do with us, nothing to do with anyone.

BEN: It is though... I mean if I'm living opposite Bates Motel then of course it's our business. The other day he had an axe... AN AXE for Christ's sake.

SOPHIE: He was probably doing a bit of gardening.

BEN: In a fourth floor flat? Must be a Hell of a window box.

SOPHIE: There will be an explanation... You've solved your own equation... Axe equals the unknown quantity.

BEN: This is serious.

SOPHIE: You're right there. Police take spying fairly seriously.

BEN: I'm not spying... You watch and you learn... I started out just watching the birds but it strikes me we're pretty much the same... It's my amphitheatre... The theatre of the street... The theatre of people. The curtains open and the performance begins and everyone has a part to play.

SOPHIE: Ben... You *will* stop all this once you're better.

BEN: Of course I will... Did you manage to get more of those painkillers?

SOPHIE: Yeah... But you go easy on them, I think they're giving you delusions. *(Looking around)* Any idea where I left my bag?

BEN: No, haven't got a clue. *(Picks up binoculars again and is watching flat opposite.)*

SOPHIE: I thought you were the master of surveillance... Where did I leave that, then?... Don't say I left it on the bus.

BEN: Wait a minute... Is it black with silver clasps?

SOPHIE: Yes, you seen it somewhere?

BEN: *(describing what he can see opposite)* Containing keys with a purple tag, white mobile...

SOPHIE: Yes, that's it.

BEN: He's got it... Your friend. *(Passes her binoculars.)* Go on, take a look.

SOPHIE: *(doesn't bother to look.)* What? The guy opposite...

BEN: Yeah.

SOPHIE: You mean he's taken my belongings off the bus?

BEN: Told you. I knew he was up to something.

SOPHIE: We'll see about that. *(Goes to door.)*

BEN: What are you doing?

SOPHIE: I'm going to go round there and get it back of course.

BEN: No Soph... Don't blow my cover.

SOPHIE: The phone then... He's got my phone... I'll ring him. *(Picks up BEN's phone and quickly dials.)* Hate to admit it, but you were right about him... *(Presumably has got through)* Hello... Yes, I'm the rightful owner of the handbag you've stolen, could you please stop going through it and give it back. *(Listens for a second and then relays conversation to BEN.)* He said he had to go through it in order to answer the phone

BEN: Like Hell, he was already going through it... I saw him.

SOPHIE: *(down phone)* Like Hell, you were already going through it.....

BEN: Tell him to keep his nose out of other people's business.

SOPHIE: Shhh. *(Listening to phone)* He says that he found it on the bus.

BEN: Why didn't he hand it in to lost property or take it to the police station?

SOPHIE: Good point. *(To phone)* Why didn't you take it to the police? *(Listens to answer.)* Right...

BEN: What did he say to that one?

SOPHIE: Apparently he's the Deputy Chief of Police.

BEN: Right... Well, I guess that does change things. God, I've been spying on the Old Bill.

SOPHIE: We've only got his word for that though, he needs to prove it.

BEN: *(sarcastic)* How are we going to do that? Get him to get his truncheon out and wave it at the window.

SOPHIE: *(starts to relay message)* Could you come to the window and get your...

BEN: *(interrupts)* No. Hold on, hold on. Don't say the *window* he'll know we're watching him from across the road.

SOPHIE: Hold that thought... I'll get back to you. *(Finishes call and puts down phone.)* What's he doing now?

BEN: *(watching through binoculars)* He's put it all back in the bag, the phone and everything. It's like he's waiting.

SOPHIE: Maybe it's innocent enough... Maybe I over-reacted. We've just picked up the wrong bags. He did have one a bit like the one that I had. I picked up his and he picked up my things.

BEN: Why was he travelling on the bus, though?

SOPHIE: Could be anything... Maybe his partner has got a muscle tear and claims she can't drive.

BEN: It's the biggest muscle tear...

SOPHIE: *(interrupting)* In the history of mankind... Yeah, I know... Look, I'm going over to get it. *(Gets coat.)*

BEN: No... Wait.

SOPHIE: You can watch out for me if you're that worried... I can be part of your drama of the streets.

BEN: Just be careful. *(SOPHIE exits and he shouts after her.)* Hold on... You forgot *his* bag... God, she's such an amateur at this. *(He thinks for a second and picks up the bag that was left behind and hobbles back to chair. He watches once more through the binoculars and talks into the voice recorder.)* 15.43 hours Sophie leaves the apartment. All quiet opposite... Suspect moves to kitchen and goes through drawers. *(Realigns binoculars)* Sophie now in street waiting for traffic. *(Temptation is too great. While he waits he opens the bag and slowly takes out a blonde wig and a blood stained green dress.)* Oh my God... Sophie *(He gets to his feet and hurries out in panic.)*

THE END

The Mysterious Case of the Brewer's Droop

by Luke Hollands

© Luke Hollands 2011

Characters
HARKER - male
ARCHIE - male
INSPECTOR BRADBY -female

Synopsis
An Edwardian super-sleuth and his partner in crime-solving, encounter clichés, melodrama and innuendos galore as they try to solve a dastardly plot to poison pints of ale.

Author
LUKE HOLLANDS is a London-based author, playwright and television producer. He learnt how to tell tall tales while interviewing politicians, celebrities and criminals as a newspaper journalist. Thinking he should get a proper job he joined the BBC. Since then he has written and produced quirky radio documentaries, made films about everything from cars to carnivorous plants and once danced on live television dressed as a giant bear. The main characters in this pint-sized play also feature in Luke's debut novel, *Peregrine Harker and the Black Death*, available from all good book shops, and some bad ones too.

Setting
Winter 1902. A lonely fishing village in South Wales. A night as dark as pitch, a thick mist rolling in off the sea. The only signs of life are the flickering lights emerging from the salt-encrusted windows of a public house. Inside the hostelry, two mustachioed men are huddled close over a table, coat collars pulled up high, hats pulled down low, their eyes shifting about the room. Each has a pint of frothy beer in front of him. Among the hubbub of the inn we can hear their clipped Edwardian voices.

HARKER: What the devil's wrong with you Archie? You've had that peculiar grimace on your face ever since we boarded the train at London.

67

ARCHIE: Harker, when you told me we were going for a pleasurable jaunt to the seaside. I thought we'd be enjoying fish and chips, sticks of rock and saucy postcards, not sat in a dingy tavern, in a desolate Welsh fishing village.

HARKER: By dingy tavern I take it you mean this quaint little inn? *(Gesturing around him)*

ARCHIE: This 'quaint little inn' as you call it, positively radiates villainy. Just look about us. I've never seen such a collection of vagabonds, villains and vagrants. Do you know, I was making my way to the WC when I swear I saw a group of men engaged in a cockfight.

HARKER: *(Sagely)* That's exactly why we're here Archie.

ARCHIE: To take part in a cockfight?

HARKER: No, my dear friend, for the villainy. Make a note of the date Archie. For this day in October 1902 will go down in history as the day we solved our most daring case. Britain may know us as the most cunning sleuths of the age, but this evening we shall secure our place in history... *(Pause)*... Did you remember to bring your revolver Archie?

ARCHIE: Yes Harker.

HARKER: Good. And the handcuffs?

ARCHIE: And the handcuffs.

HARKER: Excellent... I'm afraid we may need both before our night's work is done, for we are here to solve a most tricky case... We are here to put an end to the mystery of the brewer's droop.

ARCHIE: By Jove, Harker that sounds serious.

HARKER: It is serious Archie. Most serious indeed... I was first made aware of this particular problem by a lady of the night...

ARCHIE: Were you indeed!

HARKER: This is no time for japes Archie, the whole Empire is at stake.

ARCHIE: Apologies old boy, do continue.

HARKER: As I was saying, I was first made aware of this particular problem by a lady of the night named Nancy Turner.

ARCHIE: Not Old Nance who plies her trade at the East India Docks?

HARKER: I believe so, yes.

ARCHIE: What, bob-a-job Nance?

HARKER: That is how some of her 'suitors' refer to her, yes.

ARCHIE: The same Old Nance who can do that trick with the thrupenny bits?

HARKER: Surely you don't know of this harlot Archie?

ARCHIE: Er... No, I've never heard of her.

HARKER: I should hope so too. She is a woman of particularly loose virtue... but she has been of valuable help with some of my past enquiries. She keeps me abreast of all the comings and goings in the East End, in fact you could say she's something of an expert on the subject...

Three months ago she came to me complaining her trade had completely dried up. Naturally I dismissed her concerns. I thought nothing more of the matter until a few days later I met a medical friend of mine at the Turkish baths in Northumberland Avenue. He's something of an expert in nervous disorders, and told me a curious tale about a rapid increase in young gentleman being... how shall I put this? '...unable to fulfill their marital duties'.

ARCHIE: Ah, so that's when you sensed something was up?

HARKER: Well actually Archie that was the problem, it wasn't. After making some enquiries I learned doctors across the land were being confronted with the same problem, there had been a rise... *(Coughs awkwardly)*...or perhaps I should say increase, in problems in the trouser department. Men, who had once been famed for their 'stiff upper lip', were starting to wilt.

ARCHIE: Good grief Harker, what the Devil could be the cause?

HARKER: You won't be surprised to hear Archie I made it my mission to find out. After weeks of careful searching I discovered the problem had started at the same time a German brewer began operating a shipping route between Hamburg and Britain. It had to be more than a coincidence. I decided to travel to Hamburg to find out more. Naturally I went incognito, disguising myself as a native German.

ARCHIE: Ah, so that's why I found those leather shorts in your room?

HARKER: Er, quite... In Hamburg I managed to befriend a group of German sailors employed by this brewery; after gaining their trust they eventually allowed me access to their inner circle.

ARCHIE: *(To self)* Did they indeed... *(To Harker)* Rough work was it?

69

HARKER: You know me old boy, never averse to bending over backwards in the line of duty, especially when the future of the Empire's at stake.

ARCHIE: *(To self)* Well, I'd always had my suspicions...

HARKER: *(Ignoring Archie)* One night they let me come aboard their vessel, they wanted to show me their lower decks. What I saw took my breath away.

ARCHIE: *(To self)* I'm not sure I want to know...

HARKER: There was row upon row of British ale kegs stacked in the hold. Each one marked with a bona fide British brewer's mark. Seeing I was puzzled my new chums, taking me for a fellow German, explained why they were there. It appears I had uncovered a fiendish plot to poison the beer of Britain.

ARCHIE: *(Splutters into pint, now very interested)* Good God man, surely not even the Germans would play a dastardly trick like that?

HARKER: I'm afraid they have done old boy. They've been smuggling empty barrels of ale out of Blighty, filling them with a poisonous drop, then they return them to our shores where they go back into circulation undetected.

ARCHIE: The fiends! What exactly is this poison?

HARKER: It is the product of a new brewing technique, a particularly potent brew called Laa-ger.

ARCHIE: Laa-ger eh! What are the effects of this Laa-ger?

HARKER: Well, after a few sips the effects are hardly noticeable, but the danger comes on finishing the first pint. One begins to start feeling a sense of enormous exhilaration...

ARCHIE: Sounds fairly harmless...

HARKER: Alas it gets worse... much worse. After drinking some more one begins to loose one's solid sense of British reserve... Chaps start to get all touchy-feely with each other and go on about what good friends they are... or cry over a football or rugger match... or even worse, take to the floor of the pub and start dancing.

ARCHIE: Great Scott! Dancing you say? We can't have that, we're British.

HARKER: Indeed. But wait, there's more. After consuming copious quantities of this brew it can make one search out the nearest telegraph operator and have the fellow telegram an old flame, so you can tell the lass how much you still adore her, and how much you fancy a spot of rumpy pumpy... But that rumpy pumpy will never come because here's the rub... this laa-ger is guaranteed to make even the most stiff-upper-lipped chap wilt like a daisy when he's in the bedroom.

ARCHIE: Heavens old boy, what an underhand trick.

HARKER: Yes, indeed. Just think of the implications Archie, if our brave boys start supping on this brew the very procreation of our nation could be at stake!

ARCHIE: Well, I take it you have a cunning plan old bean?

HARKER: Yes old friend, I do. Through my investigations I have discovered the illicit kegs are being delivered through this very port, in fact this place is rife with the stuff, and tonight I mean to catch the culprits red handed. In fact I've sent word to Scotland Yard. Inspector Bradby should be here at any moment.

ARCHIE: Good show... *(Face falls, he has a thought)* But hang on old chap, if this place is rife with the stuff then couldn't it be that the very beer we're drinking now could well be laa-ger?

HARKER: Good God Archie you're right: how many have you had?

At this point ARCHIE seems to come over a little queer.

ARCHIE: I don't know Harker, but I think... I think...

HARKER: Yes?

ARCHIE: I think...

HARKER: Yes?

ARCHIE: I think... I love you

HARKER: Good God man, you've been drinking laa-ger all night! Stay strong old chap, they've got to you... *(Starts to sob a little.)* Oh how will I ever forgive myself *(starts to sob more, obviously drunk himself)*.

ARCHIE: *(Puts his arm around HARKER.)* Don't worry old bean... have I ever told you, you are the best friend ever *(slurring words heavily now)*.

HARKER: *(Now slurring words too)* No... you are.

ARCHIE: No you are...

While this inane one-upmanship continues in the background our attention is drawn to a third who has rushed hurriedly into the bar. She is INSPECTOR BRADBY and we see her searching the pub to find our inept heroes.

HARKER: *(Arm in arm with ARCHIE)* Do you know what I really fancy now?

ARCHIE: I dunno...one of those Turkish kebabs?

HARKER: No, no, no ,no... What I really fancy is...

ARCHIE: Yes?

HARKER: A dance. *(Gets down on one knee.)* Archibald... would you do me the honour of the next dance...

ARCHIE: I would indeed old boy.

Our pair of chums, drunk on lager, begin to waltz around the pub arm in arm, it is then they are noticed by the inspector.

BRADBY: *(Flabbergasted)* What the blue blazes are you two up to?

She shouts at them in a bid to catch their attention. They ignore her, they are both singing and dancing with gay abandon. It is evident the inspector has caught a whiff of their boozy breath...

BRADBY: The pair of you smell like a German brewery. I should have thought you knew better than to drink on duty Mr Harker... and I certainly expected more from you Archie.

ARCHIE: *(Mock drunken enthusiasm)* Oh hello Inspector! Are we glad to see you!

HARKER: Coo-ee!

ARCHIE: Now would you be so kind to send a telegram for me, it's to a certain lady of the East End called Nancy Turner... It goes Rumpy..stop...Pumpy...stop...

BRADBY: I'll give you Rumpy Pumpy you drunken sot!

HARKER: Will you now you saucy thing...

INSPECTOR BRADBY grabs hold of the pair, linking arms with them, getting them under control she goes to leave the pub. Suddenly she stops and looks at the audience

BRADBY: By God, you're all at it. We'd better get out of here!

INSPECTOR BRADBY manhandles our drunken pair out of the pub.

THE END

Room in the Womb

by Lou Treleaven

Characters
EGG
SPERM

Synopsis

When Egg meets Sperm they do not get off to a good start, but circumstances soon mean they must learn to get along.

Setting and Properties

This play can be performed in any setting. If possible, Sperm should be wearing goggles, snorkel and flippers.

The Author

This is Lou's third published Pint-sized Play. She also writes children's books published by Maverick Arts Publishing and plays published by Lazy Bee Scripts. Her website is loutreleaven.com

Enter EGG at a run.

EGG: Woah. Where am I? There's no way out. Great. What am I supposed to do now? Just sit around until—

Enter SPERM, out of breath. He tears off his goggles and snorkel.

SPERM: Made it! I beat the odds. Can't believe I did it. *(To EGG.)* Congratulate me, then.

EGG: On what?

SPERM: Winning! I won. Woo-hoo! Come on, this is my big moment.

EGG: What was it, some sort of novelty fun run? The flippers?

SPERM: What's wrong with the flippers? They're Winner's Flippers, that's what these are. *(Looking round.)* So this is it. The Womb. Nice ambience. Like the rhythm. Pa-dum. Pa-dum. Very reassuring. Very tribal.

EGG just glares at him suspiciously.

SPERM: Right. So. Next stage. Hi. What's a nice egg like you doing in a place like this? No? OK, erm… Heaven must be missing an egg, because… No, that doesn't work. I must be in a museum, because you're a work of art. Work of egg. The whole egg thing doesn't really work with these lines. Hi. You're an egg, and I'm—

EGG: Oh my god. Could you please go back to whatever weird body part you came from?

SPERM: You think I'm local? You have no idea.

EGG: This is a private area. Very private. You can't just burst in. And anyway, you're not… *(pointing at flippers)*. You've got…

SPERM: *(lifting flippers)* You're obsessed. Believe me, where I come from – which I stress again is definitely not local – this is normal, to the power of a hundred million. Whereas you—

EGG: Going to take the mickey because I'm round, are you? All my sisters are round. This thing we're in is round. Everything's round apart from you.

SPERM: Yeah. Yeah, I like it. I think I'm going to fit in well.

SPERM moves towards EGG.

EGG: Oh no. Get away from me, you creepy little fish.

EGG pushes SPERM, and their hands stick together.

SPERM: Too late! This is it, it's actually happening.

EGG: Make it unhappen.

SPERM: I can't. We've fused! Aren't you excited? Watch and weep, lardbuckets!

EGG: Who are you talking to? Is there someone else out there?

SPERM: Just the lads. Came with me for the ride. It's all right, they're not watching.

EGG: Watching what? Nothing's happening – oh!

Both jump.

SPERM: What did you do?

EGG: I don't know, it just sort of – ew.

SPERM: There's a kind of gooey layer around us.

EGG: Great – now we're even more 'fused'.

SPERM: Don't worry about the others. They didn't reach you in time, so they'll just wither away and die.

EGG: What?

SPERM: Yeah, they didn't fulfil their biological purpose so... *(lolls head and sticks out tongue.)*

EGG: That's harsh.

SPERM: Someone's got to win. If I hadn't made it here first I'd be a dried up old tadpole like those poor sods. You've got the best one.

EGG: Really. You said you were all identical.

SPERM: Yes, but I'm the winner, so obviously I'm faster, stronger, healthier... just generally pretty fit.

EGG: For a tadpole.

SPERM: Look, we should really try to get on, now that we've... you know. Fused. Let's get to know each other. Tell me about your family.

EGG: I don't know if I can. It's painful.

SPERM: Sorry, I'll just adjust my...

EGG: No, my story. It's tragic.

SPERM: More tragic than losing a hundred million family members in one go?

EGG: There were a hundred million of you?

SPERM: Yep. Go on.

EGG: Forget it. I obviously can't compete with your all-consuming grief.

SPERM: No, tell me. Please.

EGG: We were perfectly happy once, all snuggled up together in our little sack. And then, one day, one of us just disappeared. It happened again four weeks later. It was like we were being picked off one-by-one by some crazed murderer.

SPERM: So what happened?

EGG: I don't know. One day I was there and the next – whoosh! *(Realises)* It's happened to me, hasn't it? I've been picked off – and you're the crazed murderer!

SPERM: *(holding up flippers)* In these?

EGG: You're right. You don't look like a crazed murderer. You're more of a... an anchovy.

SPERM: Anyway, forget all that. Can't you see it was all just leading up to this moment: you and me together, here?

EGG: Did it have to?

SPERM: There's no way back so yes. Come on, you have to trust me. *(Puts arm round EGG)* Is that comfortable?

EGG: So so.

SPERM: Because I can't let go now. That gooey stuff.

EGG: No, it's OK. It is comfortable.

SPERM: Are you sure? Because I could put my other arm here— *(puts other arm round EGG)*

EGG: No, it's fine—

SPERM: Too late. Sorry.

EGG: It's fine.

Both gasp.

SPERM: Woah, did you feel that?

EGG: What?

SPERM: That tingle. You did, didn't you?

EGG: What's happening?

SPERM: I don't know.

EGG: I thought you had all the answers. When you came in here...

SPERM: That was just bravado, brought on by the rush of winning the race. Did you know that the odds against me being the one to reach you were—

EGG: Could you stop talking please? I think we're going to have another tingle.

SPERM: Sorry. I talk when I'm nervous. You should have heard me before take-off, back in the old ejector seat—

EGG: You're not scared, are you?

SPERM: Me? Scared? Shall I tell you what I think's going to happen?

EGG: OK.

SPERM: I think we're going to grow into something.

EGG: Really?

SPERM: Yeah. This is all for a reason, right? I think we're going to multiply, and those cells are going to multiply, and those cells are going to multiply, and in the end we'll become...

EGG: What? What will we become?

SPERM: A frog.

EGG: I don't want to be a frog. Get this thing off me, someone!

SPERM: Maybe not a frog then. Something even more amazing. Like... I know. A dolphin.

EGG: You weren't kidding when you said you didn't know, were you?

SPERM: No.

EGG: Wait. Something's happening.

SPERM: More tingling?

EGG: No. Different this time. I think you're right. Not about the frog. I think we are going to grow into something.

SPERM: It won't hurt, will it?

EGG: You are scared. Come here. *(Holds SPERM close.)* Nothing can hurt you. We're in this together. OK?

SPERM: You've changed.

EGG: Look who's talking.

SPERM: We've both changed. And it's only just beginning. OK, here it comes. Here comes life.

EGG: Yes, here it comes. You ready?

SPERM: Yes.

EGG: Three, two, one—

EGG & SPERM: *(expectantly)* Go.

THE END

Room in the Womb by Lou Treleaven

.

Edgeways

by Dorothy Lambert

Characters

MARCUS – a businessman, calm and very dry.
JAQUI – a woman, cringingly "caring".

The Author

DOROTHY LAMBERT has written several one-act plays for the amateur stage and two comedies *Loose Descriptions* and *A Near Miss* have been published by New Theatre Publications.

She began writing ten-minute plays for the first Pint-sized Plays Competition in 2008 and was delighted when *Chilled Wine* came third in the Script Slam. Since then *Thirty Love* (2012) and *Knight Intruder* (2013) have also been successful. Also a farce *Deadline* (2014) and a ten-minute play *Chance Encounter* (2015) each came second in Sussex Playwright's competitions.

Dorothy is married with a large and lively family and lives in Dorset.

MARCUS is sitting on the parapet (a table will serve) of a high-rise office building and gazing into the distance. JAQUI enters from the side, out of his view. She is wearing a towelling bathrobe, a shower cap and slippers. She approaches him slowly, doubled up and gasping for breath.

JAQUI: Hello there. It's all right. Keep calm. I shan't come any closer. I'm not going to touch you.

MARCUS: Good.

JAQUI: My name's Jaqui. That's with a q. J,a,q,u,i. Not ck.

MARCUS: I wasn't thinking of writing it in the diary.

JAQUI: No of course not. Would you like to tell me yours?

MARCUS: Not particularly.

JAQUI: Oh.

MARCUS: It's Marcus.

JAQUI: Well Marcus, this isn't the answer you know.

MARCUS: I'm not sure I even understand the question.

JAQUI: I know. Life can be very confusing. Would you like to tell me about it?

MARCUS: No.

JAQUI: You see I was just coming out of the shower and I looked out of the window to check if it was raining. They forecast on Local Radio that today we would have sunny spells and scattered showers.

MARCUS: Thanks for the meteorological update.

JAQUI: No, I'm just explaining that's when I saw you up here on the edge of the roof. It gave me quite a funny turn I can tell you, but I felt drawn to come to talk to you.

MARCUS: About the weather?

JAQUI: Oh dear, you're not enjoying sunny spells at the moment are you?

MARCUS: You think.

JAQUI: A trouble shared they say is...

MARCUS: A trouble doubled.

JAQUI: I don't believe that's true. A friend in need and all that.

MARCUS: Another fatuous cliché.

JAQUI: Ah bless, you are a sad old thing. I know what it's like. I feel your pain.

MARCUS: Do you.

JAQUI: Could you just turn round and face me, do you think?

MARCUS: Why?

JAQUI: So I can talk to you.

MARCUS: It hasn't stopped you so far.

JAQUI: I live across the street you see. Look, I'll show you my flat, the one with the window boxes full of red geraniums, very cheery.

JAQUI moves to the edge and points down.

Just there. Oh my God! *(Reels back in panic.)* Vertigo!

MARCUS: Vertigo? I thought you lived just across the street.

JAQUI: Yes I do. Oh, I see. How can you make a joke at a time like this?

MARCUS: It seems I can't.

JAQUI: It's such a long way up.

MARCUS: And an equally long way down.

JAQUI: Oh, don't think about that.

MARCUS: There's a great view from up here though. You can see right out as far as the ring road and the new hospital, over budget and understaffed. Conveniently close to the crematorium. You can even see the plume of smoke rising to the heavens.

JAQUI: That's awful. You mustn't dwell on that. My neighbour lost her husband in there.

MARCUS: The crematorium?

JAQUI: No, the hospital.

MARCUS: Well it's a big place.

JAQUI: No, he died! He only went in to get his bunions fixed and he caught that Zoro virus.

MARCUS: The symptoms were masked?

JAQUI: What? No, he was dead inside a week. His wife was devastated. She'd only just been to Marks and Spencer's and bought him two new pairs of pyjamas.

MARCUS: Bad luck. Still, as long as she kept the receipt.

JAQUI: Have you got something wrong with you?

MARCUS: We've all got something wrong with us.

JAQUI: Is it *(she mouths cancer)?*

MARCUS: What?

JAQUI: The big C. Is it terminal?

MARCUS: Life is terminal.

JAQUI: I'm very sorry to hear that, Martin. How long have you got, months, weeks?

MARCUS: What gave you the impression that I'm ill?

JAQUI: Well, because you're here.

MARCUS: I work here.

JAQUI: Do you? What, in these offices? It must be the redundancies then. I hear that they've sacked another fifty people this week. I lost my job here six months ago. I hate that expression, lost, it always sounds as if you carelessly left it on the bus. Not that I came on the bus of course, just walked…

MARCUS: …across the street.

JAQUI: That's right. We'll have to let you go, she said, as if they were keeping me here against my will. I loved my work. Still, look on the bright side if I hadn't been at home today I wouldn't have spotted you, would I? It's an ill wind.

MARCUS half turns his head and notices her clothing.

MARCUS: You must be cold.

JAQUI: Don't you go worrying about me. Have they given you the push? *(She gestures.)* Oh sorry that was tactless.

MARCUS: No, I'm still gainfully employed, unlike some poor sods.

JAQUI: Count yourself lucky then, and at least my husband's still in work so we've got one wage coming in. Are you married?

MARCUS: I was.

JAQUI: Oh I see. Marital problems is it? Your wife's left you has she, gone off with another man? You must be feeling so desperate and rejected, but you're still quite a reasonably attractive man and not all that old, you'll soon find that other "someone special".

MARCUS: I did.

JAQUI: What, you mean you broke up the marriage? Typical, it's always the man that cheats!

MARCUS: I think you'll find that statistics don't bear out your sweeping statement.

JAQUI: I suppose now you're ashamed of yourself and wracked with guilt.

MARCUS laughs.

JAQUI: It's not funny, Malcolm. I'm worried that my husband might be having an affair. He often has to work late and he comes home smelling of an unfamiliar perfume. When I mentioned it he said it was the air freshener they use in the rest rooms. I went and sniffed all the room fragrances they sell in Sainsbury's, I have a very good nose, but I couldn't find it at all. What do you think I should do?

MARCUS: Try Tesco's

82

JAQUI: No, I mean do you think I might be right?

MARCUS: Look, I've no idea. I don't know your husband.

JAQUI: I just thought from a man's angle…

MARCUS: It's not my problem.

JAQUI: I know it's not but perhaps…

MARCUS' mobile rings and he answers it.

RECORDED VOICE: This is an important call about your life insurance.

MARCUS: *(cancelling the call)* Piss off!

JAQUI: There's no need to take that attitude.

MARCUS: *(he glances at his watch.)* Right, time to go.

JAQUI: NOOO.

JAQUI rushes forward and grabs his arm and they both teeter on the edge before landing back on the roof.

JAQUI: Oh thank God, Michael, you're safe now.

MARCUS: Crazy woman! You almost had us both over the edge!

JAQUI: I saved your life but you don't have to thank me, I haven't really done anything special.

MARCUS: Thank you? You bloody nearly killed me! Promise me you'll never think of taking this up professionally.

JAQUI: What do you mean?

MARCUS: This counselling crap.

MARCUS pulls a cigarette packet from his pocket and moves to leave.

I only came up here for a quiet smoke but there were moments there when…

JAQUI: Don't go! What about the police?

MARCUS: You called the police? What did you say?

JAQUI: I told them that there was a desperate suicidal soul about to jump off this roof.

MARCUS: Wrong call. It was you who jumped, to conclusions.

MARCUS walks away

JAQUI: You never said.

MARCUS: You never asked.

JAQUI: They'll be here soon, can't you just…

MARCUS: What? Jump?

JAQUI: Sit on the edge again.

MARCUS: Sorry, can't stop, I've got a conference call in five minutes.

JAQUI: Look, look I can see the blue flashing lights. They're coming! What shall I say? They might think it's me!

MARCUS: Well good luck with that.

MARCUS moves further away.

JAQUI: Oh my goodness, my goodness gracious me! What am I going to do?

MARCUS: Stop running round like a headless chicken. Go home and put some clothes on.

JAQUI: But the police will be coming up here. They'll see me. Will they use the lift or the stairs do you think?

MARCUS: No idea. Both probably.

JAQUI: I can't face them, not like this. Please help me. I did come all the way up here to save your life!

MARCUS: But I wasn't intending to…

JAQUI: I still came.

MARCUS: *(turns back)* So you did. OK, Jaqui with a q. Pull yourself together. Come on, I'll show you the fire escape.

JAQUI: Thank you, Marcus.

MARCUS: Yeah! Finally you got the name right! This way. You won't enjoy it.

They both exit.

MARCUS: *(off)* Brace yourself. And hold onto the hand-rail. Don't look down!

JAQUI: *(off)* OOOH MY GOD!

THE END

To Halloumi and Back

by Simon Birkbeck

Characters
SALLY
JEAN
WAITRESS

Synopsis
Two women in a restaurant trying to order without falling out over mispronunciations.

Setting and Properties
Cafe table and chairs, menus

Author
SIMON BIRKBECK is a published author whose titles include the Goneunderland series *The Knappler's Burden* and *The Beast of Steaming Forest* with a third book to be released in 2017. Simon has been a Pint-Sized Play finalist on three occasions. From New Zealand, Simon is a former journalist having worked at several organisations including the Times and the FT. He currently works as a Senior Content Manager for a London-based creative agency.

SALLY: I think I'll have the beef burger.

JEAN: They look nice.

SALLY: Though I'm not sure.

JEAN: There's one with blue cheese. You like blue cheese.

SALLY: Where's that?

JEAN: Bottom of the burger list.

SALLY: Oh yes.

JEAN: Right, so that's chicken salad for me, beef burger with blue cheese for you and we can share a bowl of chips.

SALLY: Hang on a mo', I'm just not sure. Do I want beef? Let's see. Chicken? No. What's hallo-mee?

JEAN: Halloumi. It's a cheese.

SALLY: Is it? What's it like?

JEAN: Nice. Rubbery but nice. It's usually grilled.

SALLY: Rubbery? I don't like the sound of that.

JEAN: Well stick to your blue cheese. You like blue cheese.

SALLY: I suppose so.

JEAN: I'll grab someone...

SALLY: Wait a minute. Maybe I should try this hallo-mee. You're always saying I should try new things.

JEAN: I'm worried halloumi might be a step too far. Just stick to the meat and blue cheese.

SALLY: Doesn't the hallo-mee come with meat?

JEAN: *Halloumi*. It's usually a substitute for meat.

SALLY: No, I don't want that. I'm not having just cheese in my burger.

JEAN: You've still got everything else, lettuce, tomato, onions...

SALLY: Yes, but no meat. I mean, it's not a burger, is it?

JEAN: Right, so beef burger with blue cheese it is. Waitress...

SALLY: Just a mo', Jean. The other day Donna, you know Donna, takes those keep-fit classes, she said I should be cutting back on the processed meat. Maybe this hallo-mee is just what I need.

JEAN: Fine. Order it.

SALLY: Or was it carbs? That's it, cut down on carbs, she said. You know, bread and things. She said her and Roger had a meal without any potatoes the other week. Difficult at first, she said, but you soon get used to it. I think I'd miss my spuds. And bread. How you'd go about making a bread and butter pudding is beyond me.

JEAN: I guess you simply wouldn't have one.

SALLY: Yes, I suppose you're right.

JEAN: So do you want a burger without the buns or a burger without the meat?

SALLY: I'm not sure now. Though a burger without buns is hardly a burger either, is it?

JEAN: It's what they call a deconstructed burger.

SALLY: Desconstructed? Fancy that, they've even got a name for it. Do you think they construct the burger first then take the rolls away? No, I can't see them doing that. They probably just throw it on the plate. What do you think, Jean?

JEAN: I think I'm getting hungry.

SALLY: Sorry love, I'll make a decision. Let's see... Can you see anyone else eating hallo-mee?

JEAN: Halloumi. It's *halloumi*.

SALLY: That's what I said, harmoomlee.

JEAN: Sally, can we order?

SALLY: OK, OK, I'll make a decision. We don't want you losing your temper. Right, beef burger with blue cheese.

JEAN: Good.

SALLY: What's this? "Choose your bun".

JEAN: Christ.

SALLY: Plain, sesame seed, wholegrain, bry-otch-ee... Bryotchee, isn't that sweet?

JEAN: Brioche. Made with egg. Yes, it's a bit sweet.

SALLY: Oh no, not for me. Not with a burger. Oh Jean, look at this. They make them with cee-a-batter! Dave and I had some cee-a-batter when we were on holiday. Lovely, it was. When we told the waiter how much we liked it and could we have some more he laughed so hard I thought he was going to choke! "Cee-a-batter, madam, of course you may have some more cee-a-batter" He was lovely, he really was. Dave reckons we must have tipped him half the cost of the dinner! We went back the next night and he and his mate both waited on our table. Two of them! We were all in stitches.

JEAN: Sally...

SALLY: Sorry love. Right, I'm going to take the plunge. Hallo-mee with cee-a-batter it is. Done.

JEAN: I'll order. Waitress!

WAITRESS: Yes madam, are you ready to order?

JEAN: Yes please. We'd like one chicken salad, one *ciabatta* burger with *halloumi* and a bowl of chips to share.

WAITRESS: Sorry madam, what was the burger?

JEAN: Ciabatta with the...

WAITRESS: Chi...?

SALLY: Cee-a-batter, dear. She meant cee-a-batter.

WAITRESS: Sorry! Me and my hearing.

JEAN: With halloumi.

WAITRESS: Hal...?

SALLY: Hallo-mee. Hallo-mee, it's the cheese.

WAITRESS: No problem. Oh wait, the hallo-mee's off. Chef's run out.

SALLY: Fancy that! And after all we've been through. Not to worry dear, I'll have the beef burger with blue cheese.

WAITRESS: No problem. Lettuce and tomato in your burger?

SALLY: Yes please.

WAITRESS: Pickles?

SALLY: Well...

JEAN: No. Just say 'no'.

SALLY: What have you got?

JEAN: Dear God...

WAITRESS: Dill, gherkin and cucumber...

JEAN: We made it!

WAITRESS: ...and jalla-penises.

THE END

Tobacco Road

by Grahame Maclean

Characters
BILL – ordinary, three kids, big mortgage, on the treadmill.
JOE – a tramp, intelligent, angry, well-read but lives on the streets.

Setting and Properties
Set in a suburban street in any city.

The Author
GRAHAME MACLEAN is a composer and conductor having started his career in the theatre. He wrote the score and lyrics for the musical *Cheers Mrs. Worthington* before being invited to write and conduct for the BBC in London. Since then he has composed film and television music for producers worldwide. He was awarded the BASCA trophy for Best British Composer and was commissioned to write the finale for the Silver Jubilee of HRH Queen Elizabeth II, performed by the Hallé Orchestra, where he was presented to Her Majesty after the performance. A chance meeting with Pat McHugh and her creative writing group in 2014 led him to playwriting. He is delighted and honoured that his first play has been included in this edition of Pint-Sized Plays.

It is early afternoon and drizzling. BILL is walking down the street with a cigarette hanging out of his mouth. He is rummaging through his coat pockets having forgotten his lighter. A bearded dishevelled man, JOE, is walking towards him, head down.

BILL: *(smiling politely)* Got a light?

JOE in a toneless voice raises his eyes but keeps his head down.

JOE: Got a fag?

BILL looks puzzled.

BILL: Pardon?

JOE: *(in the same toneless voice)* Got a fag?

BILL frowns, he isn't sure if he's misheard something.

89

BILL: Err... sorry? I just said... have you got a light?

JOE: *(sarcastically)* And I said have you got a fag?

BILL starts to show the first signs of annoyance whilst trying to remain calm and polite. He takes the cigarette out of his mouth, takes a breath and speaks slowly, in a patronizing way.

BILL: *(as if to a child)* Hang on. I'm sorry if there is a misunderstanding here, but I am not a shop... I am a man who came out without a lighter. Now! Try to understand. *(Pointing)* You were the first person I saw so I asked in a *(emphasise)* polite manner, if you had a light for this *(holds up cigarette)* simple object in my hand called a *(emphasise)* cigarette.

JOE throws his arms in the air, staggers backwards and does several over the top theatrical gestures of total disbelief.

JOE: *(shouts)* Simple! SIMPLE! I'm sure Sir Walter Raleigh would love to hear that! *(Going face to face with BILL he starts to rant.)* Do you realise that in the winter of 1578 poor old Sir Walter fought his way back across the raging seas of the Atlantic with just a wet codpiece and a seagull for a compass? *(JOE is now stabbing his finger at BILL, and driving him backwards.)* Not to mention attacks from rampant sea monsters and horny mermaids going 'wooo wooo' through the fog to lure the crew away to certain death on the rocks! And did he complain? *(Shouts)* No!! Never! He just pulled into Plymouth docks, humped dirty great sacks of tobacco on to the quay, all single-handed, so the likes of you and me can enjoy a fag!! And you think that's simple!

BILL stands shocked.

JOE: *(shouts as an afterthought.)* And let's not forget the spuds!

BILL now realizes he is talking to a complete lunatic, he is embarrassed and just wants to get away.

BILL: *(starting to mumble and stutter.)* I... err... I... just wanted a light, that's all.

I'm... er... sorry... really sorry to have bothered you... Sir, so let's just leave it.

BILL tries to turn away but JOE runs in front of him and continues his animated rant.

JOE: And what about James Bonsack! He invented that dog-end you want to stuff in your gob in 1881. He slaved away for years in a smoke filled hovel, trying to invent a machine that would make your *(shouts)* simple cigarette. Eventually he perfected it, made a fortune, coughed all the way to the bank and died a week later, but does anyone remember him? No! So don't forget! *(Build the rant.)* If he hadn't invented your fag you'd have been walking along this street with a dirty great clay pipe full of soggy leaves clamped between your teeth, looking for someone with a blowlamp to get it going for you! I suppose that's simple as well? Eh? Eh?

BILL is beginning to panic and puts his hands up.

BILL: *(stuttering)* I... I'm really, really sorry I bothered you. I just wanted a light. *(Starts to search for an excuse.)* Err... but now I... don't want one! *(Forces a smile.)* So let's just forget the whole thing. OK? Goodbye.

BILL turns and starts to walk away.

JOE: *(he is now calm and looks surprised.)* Bother me? It's doesn't bother me mate. You started it.

BILL turns and looks at JOE in total shock at the sudden change in character and accusation.

BILL: What? *(Walks back to JOE in a threatening manner.)* Right! That's it. I've just about had enough of you. Now listen. I'm really sorry I asked, I really am, but now I am going to leave.

JOE, now very calm, has a genuine look of concern on his face.

JOE: *(gently)* Hang on Sir. You seem upset. Where are you going?

BILL: *(now furious and confused is nose to nose with JOE and shouting.)* Where am I going? Anywhere you aren't you furry faced dolt. All I wanted was a light and a quiet smoke, and instead I've been subjected to a barrage of information I did not bloody want by a lunatic who's eaten an encyclopaedia and smells like a man who uses a pig as a deodorant! *(Raving)* You've shouted at me, embarrassed me, and made me late for an important meeting. I've had to endure tales of rampant ship eating sea monsters, 'wooo woooing' mermaids of death, wet codpieces, roll ups and magnetic bloody seagulls, which has left me safe in the knowledge that I now know everything there is to know about Walter Bloody Raleigh, except his inside leg measurement!

JOE: *(quickly interrupts)* It was 27 inches actually Sir.

BILL: *(loses control and screams)* AHHHHHHHHHHHHH I am going to kill you!

JOE looks mortified and is genuinely surprised. He puts his hands up and offers a humble placating smile.

JOE: *(quietly)* Hang on Guv', that's not very nice. I was only being informative and friendly. Having a bit of a chat you know. Indulging in debate, social intercourse, bit of history. You know Guv'. No harm meant, live and let live. Calm calm. Nice nice. Gently gently. Pat pat. Put the kettle on. All live in total harmony Guv'.

They both stand facing each other. BILL is shaking and staring at JOE in disbelief. JOE has the look of a cowering dog. BILL, at his wits end, slowly raises his hand and looks at the unlit cigarette he is still holding. He slowly shakes his head in total defeat and holds it out to JOE.

BILL: *(sighs)* OK. Before I loose the will to live, you win. Here, take the bloody cigarette, and I hope it chokes you.

JOE: *(looking angelic)* Oh! That's so kind of you sir, but really, I couldn't.

BILL *(menacing and grabbing JOE by the throat speaks slowly.)* You asked me for a cigarette. So I am giving you a cigarette. Now listen broom face, if you do not take it I will shove it somewhere a cigarette has never been consumed from before, and I don't think you'll like it, particularly if I can get it lit first. So here, *(he holds the cigarette in front of JOE'S face)* take it!

JOE: *(simpering surprise and still held by BILL takes the cigarette)* Oh! Well, if you insist Sir. That's so very kind, you're a true gentleman Sir, if you don't mind me saying.

BILL pushes JOE away and stands defeated.

JOE: *(timid and cowering)* Would you mind if I ask you something Sir?

BILL: *(incredulous)* What?

JOE: Would you mind if I asked your name?

BILL: *(beyond belief)* My name? What do you want to know my name for?

JOE: Well I thought we could keep in touch. You know, meet up from time to time. My name's Joe by the way.

BILL: *(slowly)* Joe. I would rather repeat the journey with Sir Walter Raleigh in 1578, and be lured onto the rocks by the 'wooo woooing' mermaids, whilst a rampant sea monster chews off my leg, than ever see you again.

JOE: *(hurt)* Oh don't be like that Sir. Go on, tell me your name.

BILL: *(shakes his head in resignation, takes a deep breath, and says slowly)* OK. It's sad, wet, late, stressed, nagged, harassed, constipated, pissed off Bill.

JOE: Oh? That's a long name Sir! Would you prefer I call you *(slowly, at the same speed as BILL)* sad, wet, late, stressed, nagged, harassed, constipated, pissed off Bill? Or just Bill?

BILL is speechless and slowly shakes his head before turning slowly and walking away like a beaten man.

BILL: *(wearily)* Goodbye Joe.

JOE: *(brightly)* Goodbye Bill. I'll miss you.

BILL: I wont miss you Joe.

JOE: Oh, don't be like that Bill, surely we can be friends.

BILL: *(stops but keeps his back to JOE)* A psychopathic monkey-eating spider, who has just discovered he prefers humans, would be preferable to you Joe.

JOE: *(sadly)* OK Bill, you win.

JOE, head down, starts to walk away in the opposite direction to BILL. He stops, turns, and calls back.

JOE: *(sadly)* Excuse me Bill, before you go, can I ask you something else?

BILL: *(slowly turns to JOE)* If it's my address, piss off Joe.

JOE: No, it isn't that Bill.

BILL: *(weary sarcasm)* Is it my inside leg measurement?

JOE: No Bill.

BILL: Or perhaps my bank details?

JOE: No Bill.

BILL: *(exhausted)* OK, What is it Joe?

JOE: *(putting the cigarette in his mouth)* Have you got a light?

THE END

Tobacco Road by Grahame Maclean

The Red Panties

by Brian Coyle

© Brian Coyle 2015

Characters
MARTIN – Forties
LIZ – Forties

Synopsis
Martin and Liz have a plan to pep up their sex life, but it all goes hideously wrong. Or does it?

Setting and Props
Set in a park. A bench required and a pair of red panties.

Author
BRIAN COYLE is a playwright based in Bristol and SE London. His plays have been performed in London, Bristol, Bath, Liverpool, Manchester and Wales. They include *Welcome To Paradise Road*, a drama about creeping state control and our surveillance society. In 2016 it won Best Script in Festival at the Page to Stage Theatre Festival in Liverpool. In 2014 he was one of the winners of the British Theatre Challenge, an international one-act play competition. In 2014 he was a runner up in Pint-Sized Plays and in 2015 he was a winner.

MARTIN *is sitting on a park bench. He looks around. He's waiting for someone. A few seconds later* LIZ *enters. She sees* MARTIN *and sidles over towards him. He glances over at her.*

LIZ: Is it free?

MARTIN: Yeah... sure... help yourself.

She sits. They look around awkwardly.

It's a nice day for it.

LIZ: What?

MARTIN: You know...

LIZ: Do I?

They sit for a few further seconds.

95

"Fall, leaves, fall; die, flowers, away; Lengthen night and shorten day."

MARTIN: You what?

LIZ: The leaves. On the ground.

MARTIN: Oh right… the leaves…

LIZ: It's a poem.

MARTIN: A poem. I see… A poem…

Do you come here often?

She stands up in disgust.

What?

She sits back down.

LIZ: Nothing.

MARTIN: Well, do you?

LIZ: No, I don't.

MARTIN: Right.

The leaves… very good.

Even more awkward.

LIZ: My name's Penelope by the way.

MARTIN: What…? Oh… right Penelope.

LIZ: And you?

MARTIN: Me? Steven… I mean Steve.

LIZ: Which?

MARTIN: Steve. Call me Steve.

LIZ: Steve. Right. Good. Nice to meet you Steve.

They awkwardly shake hands.

MARTIN: Penelope. I like that. I thought I recognised you.

LIZ: I'm a novelist.

MARTIN: Ah…That'll be it then. A novelist. I've probably seen you on the telly. Would I have read… ?

LIZ: Probably not. I write women's novels. A bit racy. Well, actually, very racy.

MARTIN: Like what's-its-name… you know…

LIZ: Yes. A bit like that.

MARTIN: Ah… No then. Probably not…

LIZ: No. And you?

MARTIN: I'm… an architect.

LIZ: Really?

MARTIN: Yes.

LIZ: Fine.

MARTIN: What?

LIZ: Fine… fine. Brutalist?

MARTIN: You what?

LIZ: Is your style brutalist? You know; lots of concrete.

MARTIN: No not brutalist. More refined, gentle like…

LIZ: Gentle… right. And would I know any of your buildings – Steve?

MARTIN: Umm… probably not.

LIZ: No go on, try me.

MARTIN: Well, you know the Shard?

LIZ: The Shard!

MARTIN: Well obviously that's not mine. I do smaller ones. Smaller shards.

LIZ: Really…

MARTIN: Yeah.

LIZ: Smaller shards?

MARTIN: That's right.

She stands up, disgusted.

LIZ: Enough, enough… I've had enough.

MARTIN: What?

LIZ: You're useless Martin. Smaller *shards*? Is that the best you can come up with?

MARTIN: What?

LIZ: Forget it.

MARTIN: I thought it was going well.

LIZ: This is a hopeless idea.

MARTIN: Penelope the novelist?

LIZ: And…?

Beat.

MARTIN: At least we tried it. We can cross that one off the list. I never wanted to be an architect anyway. I don't know why I even said it.

They sit for a few seconds.

It's nice park this isn't it? We don't come here often enough. We used to. Remember? We used to come here all the time… Do you remember that day Jamie fell off his bike and cut his eye. He screamed his head off. It looked worse that it was.

LIZ: I remember you nearly fainted when you saw that blood on his face.

MARTIN: No I didn't.

LIZ: Yes you did.

MARTIN: Well. I was worried.

LIZ: Have you heard from him recently?

MARTIN: No. Nothing. Have you heard from Ella?

LIZ: Not a thing…It's like we don't exist. Anyway.

MARTIN: What?

LIZ: Onwards.

He just looks at her.

You know.

MARTIN: Oh that.

LIZ: Well…?

MARTIN: I did it.

LIZ: You did it? Really!

MARTIN: I just said so.

LIZ: Martin Rogers. I never thought you had it in you.

MARTIN: What do you mean by that?

LIZ: You've never stolen anything in your life.

MARTIN: I have. As a kid.

LIZ: Rubbish. So? Show me then.

MARTIN: Not here.

LIZ: Yes here. Go on.

MARTIN *takes a pair of red panties out of his pocket.*

LIZ: Martin! I'm shocked. Give us a look.

MARTIN: Not in public.

She pulls them off him.

Hey you. Give 'em back...

For the next few seconds they pull at the panties. She thinks it's funny. He's mortified.

Liz... stop it.

LIZ: OK, OK. Have them. If they're so important to you.

He stuffs them in his pocket.

Red panties. I would never in a hundred years thought you'd go for something like that. Stealing a pair of red panties.

MARTIN: Well... you don't know everything about me.

LIZ: Exactly. That's the point of it. That's the whole point.

MARTIN: I know what the point is. This isn't right you know.

LIZ: What isn't?

MARTIN: It doesn't say anywhere in the book you should do anything illegal.

LIZ: No... but it says you should do something exciting... risky. It was a test.

MARTIN: A test... What do you mean by that?

Beat.

LIZ: Were you excited then?

MARTIN: What?

LIZ: Stealing them. Did it turn you on?

MARTIN: No it didn't. I was terrified.

LIZ: It's meant to turn you on.

MARTIN: Well it didn't.

LIZ: Oh yeah. Is that right? Why then?

MARTIN: What do you mean?

LIZ: You could have stolen anything: A magazine. A packet of polo mints. Why those?

MARTIN: Well, the whole point of all this is… you know—

LIZ: I don't think they'll fit me. You'll have to go back and steal another pair.

MARTIN: No way! I'm never going back in that shop again.

Beat.

LIZ: You did, take precautions? Like I told you.

MARTIN: Umm… yeah of course I did.

LIZ: Kept your back to the CCTV camera. You did remember didn't you?

He looks distracted.

Martin? Martin!

MARTIN: I was nervous. I just wanted to get in and get out.

LIZ: You're useless. You can't even steal a pair of panties without messing it up.

MARTIN: You don't think they could trace me do you? Maybe I could take them back. Put them back before they find out.

She just looks at him.

LIZ: I sometimes wonder how we ever ended up together. I do. I sometimes wonder: what would have happened if you hadn't stood on my toe in that bar.

MARTIN: *(he's been distracted.)* Maybe you could put them back for me.

LIZ: Forget about that. You'll be fine. I think this might be a waste of time. A complete waste of time.

MARTIN: I told you that. It's just a load of self-help rubbish.

LIZ: I don't mean the book Martin…

Pause.

MARTIN: I heard them at it last night.

LIZ: Who?

MARTIN: Them next door. At number 22.

LIZ: I never heard a thing.

MARTIN: At it for hours they were. We were never that noisy.

LIZ: Yes we were.

MARTIN: Were we?

LIZ: You know we were.

MARTIN: *(he thinks.)* I guess we were…

LIZ: She looks as if she's never had a shag in her life. It just shows, you never can tell. Hey. Do you remember that holiday we had in Bulgaria? We were young and skint. Sunny Days Resort. I don't think we left the room for the entire seven days we were there.

MARTIN: I remember.

LIZ: What's happened to us? We're like two completely different people. We've spent all these years bringing up two kids and in the meantime…

MARTIN: Liz don't. Not again.

LIZ: We were OK when they were at home. We were fine. But now they've gone… Why can't they just come back?

MARTIN: They can't come back… You know that. I'm glad they're gone.

LIZ: How can you say that?

MARTIN: They need to get on with their lives.

LIZ: Are you saying you don't miss them? I don't understand you anymore.

MARTIN: We've been saying for years all the things we could do when they were gone. We had plans.

LIZ: Yeah what were they again?

MARTIN: Umm… I can't remember. Anyway. We're moving on now. We have the book.

LIZ: Ah yes, the book… What a useless exercise that's been.

MARTIN's *phone goes off. It's a text.*

Who is it?

MARTIN: Nobody. A work thing.

LIZ: I thought it might be Jamie.

MARTIN: Or Ella…

LIZ: Anyway. We should probably try at least one more thing? Give it one last chance...

MARTIN: What?

LIZ: From the book I mean.

MARTIN: Oh… right.

Beat.

You haven't asked me why I was awake last night.

LIZ: Listening to them next door weren't you?

MARTIN: No, I was awake anyway. I was looking out the window. It was a clear night. I was looking at the stars.

I used to show them him the night sky. I'd point out the planets. They were interested in it.

LIZ: Just as well. It bores me to death.

MARTIN: I was looking at Jupiter and I started to cry. I don't know why.

LIZ: Martin.

MARTIN: Stupid isn't it?

LIZ: I knew it. I knew you missed them as much as I do.

MARTIN: We're meant to be the adults. But all I feel is an enormous hole now they've gone… I'm scared Liz.

And that's not the only reason I was crying. Losing them is bad enough, but…

LIZ: Oh you… come here.

She kisses him.

That was more like it. You're beginning to sound like your old self again.

MARTIN: Am I?

They sit for a couple of seconds.

LIZ: It's a nice time of year this. A nip in the air. The leaves falling. "Every leaf speaks bliss to me, Fluttering from the autumn tree."

MARTIN: That's nice.

LIZ: I like just sitting here. We should do it more often.

MARTIN: I agree. We should…

LIZ: And you with your panties in your pocket.

MARTIN: Ah… those.

Beat.

LIZ: It's a big change them going. We need to give it time. I think we'll be fine.

MARTIN: Will we?

Pause.

LIZ: Hey, you'll like this. Jane, from over the road, she told me she's been buying stuff. Good stuff from the Esso garage – from under the counter.

MARTIN: Good stuff?

LIZ: You know: Elephant, fatty, gage, goody-goody…

MARTIN *looks confused.*

Ganja!

MARTIN: Oh… right.

LIZ: I could get us some.

MARTIN: We haven't smoked that for….

LIZ: We had great sex on that. The best ever.

MARTIN: I don't know… the book says—

LIZ: Fuck the book Martin. The book is going in the bin. We know this works.

MARTIN: We did have some good times.

LIZ: I'll nip in later. And we can smoke it with impunity. No interference from nosy children. Well?

MARTIN: If you gave me enough time I could probably think of a reason why not. But right now I can't.

LIZ: Good. Come here then.

They embrace.

One thing.

MARTIN: What?

LIZ: If you do steal anymore underwear. Could you make it comfortable? I can't stand that type of stuff.

MARTIN: Who said the panties were for you anyway?

LIZ: What?

MARTIN: There are loads of things you don't know about me.

THE END

Writers' Group

by Tom Jensen

Characters
WILL – bearded writer
HARRY – writer/actor
TANYA – writer/actress

Synopsis
Will takes his play to the local writers' group, where Harry and Tanya suggest some radical improvements.

Setting And Properties
A room with three chairs.
Props: coats, a bag, scripts, a water bottle, a pen and paper, a copy of Playwriting for Dummies, a skull or a white football or balloon with skull features, a spade.

The Author
TOM JENSEN works as a French translator in London and writes absurdist drama. His short plays have been performed in the UK and abroad, and he recently completed the Royal Court writing programme. His comedy *Merger Talks* came second in the 2009 Pint-Sized Plays Script Slam and was published in the first anthology; *Writers' Group* made it to the 2016 finals, which he was delighted to attend. Tom still enjoys the occasional pint but is now also working on a barrel-sized play. You can find out more about his work at www.tomjensen.co.uk and on Twitter @absurdistworld.

A room with three chairs, coats hanging over them. WILL, HARRY and TANYA are standing, holding scripts.

They look up, then put the scripts down.

TANYA: Phew! Talk about a marathon!

WILL: Cheers guys!

HARRY: I reckon we deserve a rest.

They wander around, shaking their limbs.

TANYA: Tough sharing 19 parts, eh?

HARRY: Still, we brought the characters to life.

WILL: We certainly did!

HARRY does stretches; TANYA rearranges her hair; WILL drinks from a water bottle.

TANYA: How are we doing for time, Harry?

HARRY: *(looks at watch)* Jeez, it's nearly midnight!

TANYA: Let's crack on with the feedback.

WILL: OK.

They sit down. HARRY and TANYA pick up the scripts. WILL gets out a pen and paper.

HARRY: *(browses)* Interesting play, Will.

TANYA: Where do you see it going?

WILL: Well, I'm hoping to get it staged.

HARRY: Cool... Good to be ambitious.

TANYA: Any particular venue?

WILL: No, just... sending it off, really.

HARRY and TANYA glance at each other.

TANYA: Will, I... have to be frank with you.

WILL: Sure, go ahead.

TANYA: Getting this staged... It's wishful thinking.

WILL: Really? Wh... what's wrong with it?

TANYA: The whole story needs rethinking.

HARRY: *(nods)* It's the oldest plot in the book.

TANYA: Young man avenges father's murder...

HARRY: That's been used a lot.

TANYA: And the Oedipus thing, and the madness...

HARRY: Psychoanalysis is so dated.

TANYA: Plus, the hero should be more rounded.

HARRY: More three-dimensional.

TANYA: And where does the girlfriend fit in?

HARRY: It could be a great love story, but his mind's in the clouds.

TANYA: They don't even get a sex scene.

HARRY: And then she drowns!

WILL: *(notes this down.)* You're right.

TANYA: Secondly, you cram too much in.

HARRY: Yeah, classic mistake.

TANYA: It's trying to be a ghost story, a murder mystery...

HARRY: Even a play within a play.

TANYA: It's over-ambitious.

HARRY: Self-indulgent.

WILL: *(notes this down.)* Yes.

TANYA: Rule is, keep it simple.

HARRY: And listen to the experts... Have you got that book, Tanya?

TANYA: Yeah! *(Takes book from bag.)* Playwriting for Dummies.

HARRY: Could he hear some now, to get an idea?

TANYA: Sure. *(Browses)* Let's see... "Show don't tell."

HARRY: If we can't see the pirates attacking, cut the episode.

WILL notes this down.

TANYA: *(browses)* I love this one. "Write what you know".

HARRY: Have you ever lived in Denmark?

WILL shakes his head.

HARRY: I rest my case.

WILL nods and notes this down.

TANYA: See? Piece of cake. *(Gives WILL the book.)*

WILL: Thank you! *(Browses.)*

HARRY and TANYA get up and wander round, glancing from WILL to each other.

HARRY: Best bet's to rewrite the whole thing.

TANYA: Tear it up. Start from scratch.

HARRY: And give them exciting things to do!

TANYA: How about Hamlet murders his own father?

HARRY: And his mum takes revenge on him!

TANYA: *(claps)* Genius!

HARRY: You can keep... five characters, max.

TANYA: Yeah, scrap the minor ones like... *(clicks fingers.)*

HARRY: Rosenstern.

TANYA: And Guildencrantz.

WILL: *(notes this down.)* OK.

HARRY: And cut the clichés!

TANYA: You've got so many!

HARRY: To the manner born...

TANYA: In a nutshell...

HARRY: Hoist with his own petard...

WILL: Of course – sorry!

TANYA: It's all right! We're all on a learning curve.

WILL takes notes.

HARRY: It's depressing, too.

TANYA: You've got to remember your audience.

HARRY: The last thing they want is murder and suicide.

WILL: But what about the bit where—

TANYA: "To be or not to be"?

HARRY: Out of the question.

WILL notes this down.

TANYA: What you need is comedy.

HARRY: Slapstick, jokes...

TANYA: You can have death – just liven it up a bit.

HARRY: Take that skull scene...

TANYA: (covers face) Oh, God!

HARRY: How about doing it this way?

HARRY fetches a spade and a skull. WILL stands up, and HARRY hands him the spade.

HARRY: Here's what you've got now: *(holds up skull)* "Alas! Poor Yorick…"

TANYA: Boring!

HARRY: It's just talking heads.

WILL: But there's action too… He fights her brother—

TANYA: It's too late by then!

HARRY: Try this. Ophelia's in the cemetery, about to date Hamlet…

TANYA: She could have a musical solo…

HARRY: Yeah! Then she slips on a banana skin…

TANYA: *(mimes slipping onto her back.)* Falls into the grave and dies.

HARRY: Hamlet arrives, plays cricket with the gravedigger…

He bowls the skull at WILL, who involuntarily bats it back with the spade.

HARRY: Does a flying catch… *(Catches the skull.)* And falls in after her!

He lies on top of TANYA.

TANYA: I like it!

HARRY: See? It's got everything…

TANYA: Slapstick, tragedy, sport…

HARRY: Even necr-Ophelia!

TANYA: *(laughs)* Harry!

HARRY: My inspiration!

They are about to kiss when they remember WILL. They get up and brush themselves down.

WILL: That's **so** helpful! *(Sighs happily)* Thank you both.

TANYA: Our pleasure.

HARRY: All in a day's work.

They return to the chairs.

TANYA: We'd better be getting home.

They put on their coats and prepare to leave, turning off the lights.

HARRY slaps WILL on the back.

HARRY: Keep writing though, Will.

TANYA: Yeah, you're getting there...

HARRY: *(stifling laughter)* Slowly but surely.

TANYA: One day you might do an OK play.

WILL: Do you think so?

HARRY and TANYA: *(together)* Yeah!

WILL: Aw, thanks!

HARRY and TANYA put their arms around each other. They exit.

THE END

A Good Innings

by Barry Wood

© Barry Wood 2016

Characters
ST. PETER – any age.
COLIN INNINGS – 40+.
ELIZABETH – any age.

Synopsis
Recently deceased Colin Innings is being interviewed by an eccentric St Peter, who's determined to have a little fun with his latest applicant.

Setting and Properties
Table with two chairs positioned on the opposite sides. Files, a coin.

The Author
BARRY WOOD is an amateur playwright living in Lincolnshire with his wife and three teenage children. He started writing plays two years ago and recently played Richard III, (Romeo's brother, and Lady Macbeth's son) in a Shakespearean pantomime he wrote, available on 'Lazy Bee Scripts.' He would like to dedicate *'A Good Innings'* to his Mum who sadly passed away last year. He thinks her meeting with St Peter would have gone OK – after all she wasn't a pastry chef.

PETER is sitting at a table, with a file of papers in front of him. COLIN enters apprehensively and PETER stands up.

PETER: Mr Innings isn't it? *(Putting out his hand to greet COLIN.)*

COLIN: *(nervously)* Yes.

The two men shake hands.

PETER: Have a seat, please. We might be here some time, judging by the size of your file.

Both men sit down and PETER opens up the file.

PETER: You've obviously had an eventful life. *(Chuckling to himself)* ' A good innings' so to say. Sorry I couldn't help myself. I bet you've heard that one before?

COLIN: You could say that.

PETER: Apologies Trevor, apologies. You don't mind if I call you Trevor do you?

COLIN: No, not really – but my name is Colin.

PETER: Colin? *(Looking at the front of the file)* Sycamore Drive?

COLIN: No, Tennyson Avenue – 15 Tennyson Avenue.

PETER: Whoops! *(Shouting)* Elizabeth! *(To COLIN)* Sorry about that. Just as well though; Trevor Innings was a city banker, he'll be going straight to Hell.

COLIN: Oh yes. I think I saw him in the waiting area, punching a kitten.

PETER: Yeah, that'll be him.

ELIZABETH enters, looking irritated.

ELIZABETH: What is it now, Peter?

PETER: *(taken aback by her manners)* You've erm, given me the wrong file *(handing it to her).*

ELIZABETH: *(snatching the file)* Well excuse me! Perhaps if I'd had a break this morning, I wouldn't be making mistakes.

PETER: Perhaps, if you hadn't upset Maria yesterday, she would have turned up for work today.

(ELIZABETH storms off.)

PETER: *(to COLIN)* Sorry you had to witness that.

COLIN: That's OK. Erm, I thought you'd be all computerised.

PETER: We tried a few years ago, but Satan hacked into the system, and we inadvertently let in three serial killers, a dictator, and a couple of pastry chefs.

COLIN: What's so bad about pastry chefs?

PETER: *(firmly)* I just don't like them. *(Rubbing his fingers and thumbs together.)* With their floury little fingers…Nasty!

ELIZABETH enters with Colin's file and throws it on Peter's table.

ELIZABETH: Maria misfiled it – So she's not so perfect after all.

PETER: I never said she was perfect.

ELIZABETH: You didn't have to. I've seen the way you look at her.

PETER: All I said, was that I thought she was wearing a nice dress.

ELIZABETH: You never compliment me on my clothes.

PETER: Elizabeth, can we deal with this later?

ELIZABETH huffs and exits.

COLIN: *(to ELIZABETH as she exits)* Nice dress, by the way.

ELIZABETH: *(muttering)* Creep.

PETER: Right, back to business. *(Flicking through the file)* Let's have a look at the highlights shall we? *(Finding a certain page, he starts reading to himself.)* Now this is interesting: It says here that a couple of years ago, you pulled a pregnant woman out of a burning car.

COLIN: *(feigning embarrassment)* Yes. Yes I did.

PETER: Very impressive Colin, that certainly goes in your fav… Oh! Hang on! Apparently, you caused her car to catch fire when you crashed into it. Well that's a different story, isn't it?

COLIN: It wasn't my fault. It was an accident. I swerved to avoid hitting…something.

PETER: What?

COLIN: Erm. A cardinal.

PETER: *(incredulously)* A cardinal?

COLIN: Yeah, you know, one of those special bishop people that choose the pope?

PETER: *(leafing through the file)* I can't see any mention of that here. So, was this cardinal driving another car?

COLIN: Driving? No, no, he was wandering – in the middle of the road – in all his ecclesiastical regalia. I didn't see him at first because it was dark, but I caught a glimpse of his red gown, just in time.

PETER: So what was a cardinal doing, wandering in the road – at night?

COLIN: Not sure…Oh yeah, I think there was a care home nearby and he'd slipped out.

PETER: A care home for cardinals?

COLIN: Not just cardinals. Other members of the catholic church as well: priests, nuns. In fact, I remember seeing a couple of nuns hiding behind a tree, just before the accident. They must have been following the cardinal.

PETER: Come on Colin, level with me. *(Pointing at the file)* It says here you had twice the legal limit of alcohol in your bloodstream, the night of the accident. Be honest, there was no cardinal was there?

COLIN: Not even a little one? *(Pause. With resignation)* No, I caused the accident; I'd had a bit too much to drink. But I didn't have to pull the woman out the car – that must count for something?

PETER: So what else do we have in your favour? *(Looking back at the file)* Oh, you went to church regularly: that's good.

COLIN: Every Sunday, without fail.

PETER: Yes, every Sunday, for... Oh – for the past three months. *(Flicking through the file)* But not before. So why just the past three months?

COLIN shrugs suspiciously.

PETER: Nothing to do with the fact that it was three months ago the doctors gave you the diagnosis?

COLIN: What diagnosis was that?

PETER: You know; the one about the terminal illness?

COLIN: *(thinking)* Oh that one – yeah thinking about it, it was about that time. *(Pause)* Look, the doctors said I had twelve months to live – so I was prepared to go to church every week for a whole year.

PETER: *(not convinced)* Mmmm. *(Looking through the paperwork)* So what else do we have?

COLIN: I regularly give to charity.

PETER: Really? Oh well that's good. So who do you help support?

COLIN: Every month I donate to a sanctuary for deaf-blind, orphaned diabetic donkeys.

PETER: *(dubious)* OK – so what made you choose that charity in particular?

COLIN: I just thought, pound for pound, my money was going to the greatest number of good causes.

PETER: I see – and how much did you give?

COLIN*: (dismissively)* I'm not sure.

PETER: *(consulting the file)* Two pounds a month, for the past *(pause)* three months. So six pounds then?

COLIN: *(defensively)* Six pounds buys a lot of sugar cubes for those poor donkeys.

PETER: I thought you said they were diabetic?

COLIN: *(deflated)* Oh yeah.

Pause

PETER: Let's move on to some serious business. How are you with the Ten Commandments?

COLIN: OK. I think. I'm not sure I can remember all ten.

PETER: *(leafing through the file)* Well, from what I've seen, you should be all right with most of them. *(Looking up from the notes)* Have you ever worked on the Sabbath?

COLIN: Sunday? No I've never worked on a Sunday.

PETER: Good, very good... Ever murdered anyone?

COLIN: Certainly not!

PETER: Excellent. You're on a roll here, Colin. *(Looking back at the file)* Have you ever coveted your neighbour's ox?

COLIN: Eh? No, I've never had a neighbour with an ox.

PETER: What about a fox? Have you ever had a neighbour with a fox that you liked the look of?

COLIN: What? No. What's that got to do with anything?

PETER: What about Malcolm?

COLIN: Malcolm Tindale? He never had a fox, or an ox.

PETER: No, but he did have a nice – roof box.

COLIN looks puzzled.

PETER: *(referring to the paperwork)* According to your file, about a year ago, you said to your wife 'Carol,' and I quote, 'Have you seen the new roof box Malcolm's got on his car? It's a corker. I wish I had a roof box like that.'

COLIN: But that's not an ox. I didn't covet my neighbour's ox.

PETER: Didn't you get the memo? They've updated the tenth commandment to include anything that rhymes with ox.

COLIN: What? No. No I didn't get the memo! You're having a laugh.

PETER: *(bursts out laughing)* You're right. I'm just yanking your chain, Colin. *(Taking his glasses off, he carries on chuckling as he wipes his eyes.)* You should have seen your face.

COLIN: *(annoyed)* Jesus Christ.

PETER: *(suddenly serious)* I beg your pardon? *(Putting his glasses back on)* You were doing so well Colin – but you've just broken the third commandment: Thou shalt not take the Lord's name in vain.

Picking up a pen, PETER makes a note in COLIN'S file.

PETER: Right. Is there anything you wish to add before I make my judgement on you?

COLIN: *(nervously)* No. I don't think so.

Pause.

PETER: *(closing the file and looking up at COLIN)* Mmm. Now then. *(Sitting back, he sighs.)* You've certainly given me quite a conundrum. On the one hand, with your: heroism, charitable support and regular church attendance, you've proved that you are worthy of spending eternity in Heaven. But on the other hand, with your: drink-driving, blasphemy and roof box coveting, maybe you should burn in the eternal flames of Hell.

COLIN: You said you were joking about the roof box?

PETER: Oh yeah. But still, you haven't given much to charity, and you only went to church a few times. It's certainly a tricky one. *(Thinking)* What to do? What to do? *(Thinking)* No, I can't decide: I'm going to have to toss a coin.

COLIN is looking very agitated as PETER stands and roots in his pockets for a coin.

PETER: I'm sure I had some change somewhere. Have you got a coin?

COLIN pats his pockets and shakes his head.

PETER: Oh! Wait a minute. *(Peering around the side of COLIN'S head)* What's that behind your ear?

Grinning, with slight-of-hand, PETER 'discovers' a coin behind COLIN'S ear.

PETER: Look what I've found!

He smiles and waits for appreciation for his trick.

COLIN: *(exasperated)* Will you just get on with it? The suspense is killing me.

PETER: *(laughing)* You're already dead Colin.

COLIN: *(begging)* Please, please, I can't stand it any longer.

PETER: All right. Easy, Tiger. *(Preparing to toss the coin)* OK, heads or tails?

COLIN: Erm, heads!

PETER: Tails never fails?

COLIN: You think I should go for tails?

PETER: It's up to you.

COLIN: *(very stressed)* OK, I'll have tails.

PETER: Right. So if it's tails you get into Heaven, but heads, and you burn in Hell. Tails, you go to Heaven; heads, you burn in Hell. *(Saying it in a sing-song way while doing a little dance.)* 'Tails you go to Heaven; heads you burn in Hell. Tails you...'

COLIN: *(screaming)* Just toss the bloody coin!

PETER: Oooooo! Keep your hair on.

COLIN starts sobbing.

PETER: *(relenting)* All right. Here we go.

PETER tosses the coin. Then when he examines it on the back of his hand, he slowly looks up at COLIN. COLIN'S anxiety levels are very high. PETER looks at Colin and a sad expression starts to form on PETER'S face, as he slowly shakes his head.

COLIN: *(dropping to his knees)* No! Please! No! No!

PETER: *(his expression brightens suddenly.)* It's all right Colin, I'm just messing with you, it's tails.

All the time PETER has the coin on the back of his hand, in front of him. COLIN stops crying and looks up, shocked, but happy.

COLIN: It is?

PETER: No it's heads, you're going to Hell.

COLIN breaks down again.

PETER: I'm joking, I'm joking, it's tails.

COLIN stops crying, confused.

PETER: Or is it?

COLIN: *(hysterically)* What the hell's wrong with you, *(Lurching towards PETER)* Let me see that coin. *(Examining the coin on the back of PETER'S hand, his face lights up.)* It really is tails!

PETER proceeds to show COLIN the other side of the coin.

PETER: Actually, this coin has tails on both sides, see. *(Grinning)* I'd already decided to let you in to heaven before I tossed it.

COLIN: What? You're sick!

PETER: *(still smiling)* It was just a bit of fun, Colin. *(Gesturing with his thumb.)* Come on in.

COLIN heads off into Heaven, laughing maniacally. ELIZABETH enters holding another file.

ELIZABETH: He seemed somewhat… Unhinged.

PETER: I think I might have pushed him a bit too far.

ELIZABETH: You haven't being playing with your trick coin again, have you?

PETER: *(raising his eyes suspiciously)* Maybe.

ELIZABETH shakes her head, disapprovingly.

Pause.

ELIZABETH: Erm, about earlier.

PETER: Yes?

ELIZABETH: I might have over-reacted a little.

PETER: A little?

ELIZABETH: Sorry, Peter.

PETER: That's all right. *(Pause)* So who have we got next?

ELIZABETH: *(opening the file)* Audrey Moreau. A nurse who worked for Médecins Sans Frontières, in various war zones.

PETER: *(impressed)* I see. So how did she die?

ELIZABETH: She was killed trying to protect a young boy in a wheelchair, from a sniper.

PETER: Well, I don't think it'll be difficult to decide where she's going.

ELIZABETH: *(apprehensively)* Erm, it also says here, that she's a fully qualified pastry chef.

PETER stands, suddenly livid.

PETER: SHE CAN GO TO HELL!

THE END

Survey

by Hugh Smith

Characters
WAITRESS – young
CUSTOMER – female, slightly older

Synopsis
A customer in a café is asked to take part in a survey.

Setting and Properties
A café with a table and two chairs. There is a tablecloth and a menu on the table. Also required are a handbag, a waitress's apron, two mobile phones, a tea towel and a pair of scissors.

The Author
HUGH SMITH has written sketches for television shows including *The Russ Abbot Show*, *Hale and Pace*, *Smith and Jones* and shows on German, Belgian, Swedish and Welsh television. He has recently started writing short pieces for the stage and was delighted when *Survey* won Best Performance in the Pint-sized Plays Script Slam in 2016. He lives in Oxfordshire.

WAITRESS is tidying the table when CUSTOMER carrying handbag enters. WAITRESS stops, tucks tea towel into her apron and turns to greet CUSTOMER.

WAITRESS: Good morning, madam and welcome to the Riverside Café.

CUSTOMER: Good morning.

CUSTOMER sits at table, puts handbag down on floor and picks up menu to read.

CUSTOMER: Now then. What shall I have?

WAITRESS: I wonder, madam, if you'd be willing to take part in a short survey about your experience today at the Riverside Café?

WAITRESS produces mobile phone from pocket.

CUSTOMER: Well, I haven't actually ordered anything yet.

WAITRESS: I know, madam. The survey is on how well I said 'Good morning, madam and welcome to the Riverside Café'. It should only take about twenty minutes.

CUSTOMER: I don't think so, thank you. I'm in a bit of a hurry.

WAITRESS: But it's your chance to let us know how sincere you felt I was being. Was I putting the emphasis on the right words? Are there more appropriate words I should be using? Should I have said them in a different order? That sort of thing. How can we improve? You tell us.

CUSTOMER: Everything was fine, thank you. And anyway I hardly think a simple greeting justifies a twenty-minute survey.

WAITRESS: In that case, would you be willing to let us know why you don't think a simple greeting justifies a twenty-minute survey? By means of a short survey. It should only take about seventeen minutes.

CUSTOMER: You're having a laugh.

WAITRESS: I can assure you, madam, that we are not in the habit of having a laugh when it comes to the important matter of surveys. Although having a laugh is of course permitted in the 'Having a Laugh' seating area (*indicates seating area*). Perhaps you'd be willing to take part in our survey for people who don't like surveys?

CUSTOMER: This is ridiculous. But I'll tell you what I'll do. I'll take part in your survey if you take part in mine.

CUSTOMER reaches down and removes mobile phone from handbag.

WAITRESS: You have a survey, madam?

CUSTOMER: Oh yes. Ah ha! Weren't expecting that, were you? I'll ask you a question from my survey and then you can ask me a question from your survey.

WAITRESS: This is all highly irregular. I'm sure head office wouldn't approve.

CUSTOMER: It's up to you.

WAITRESS: Oh... all right then.

CUSTOMER: I'll let you go first.

WAITRESS: Thank you. Are you ready?

CUSTOMER: Yes. Was that the first question?

WAITRESS: No. I was just checking if you were ready. Question one (*looks at mobile phone*). Oh. Actually, that was the first question. (*Reads*) 'Are you ready? Yes, No or Don't know.'

CUSTOMER: Don't know.

WAITRESS: But just now you said you were ready.

CUSTOMER: Ah, but that was before I knew that 'don't know' was an option. My turn. (*Reads from mobile phone*) Should I have a tattoo?

WAITRESS: A tattoo? What kind of survey is this?

CUSTOMER: Just answer the question, please.

WAITRESS: Erm... no. I mean yes. Well, why don't you compromise and have it done in invisible ink?

CUSTOMER: That's not a bad idea. I'll make a note of that (*taps into mobile phone*). This could be useful after all.

WAITRESS: Right. Back to my survey. (*Reads*) Question two. On a scale of one to ten how annoying is being asked to rate things on a scale of one to ten?

CUSTOMER: Ten. (*Reads*) Should I become a Buddhist?

WAITRESS: Why not? You only live once. (*Reads*) On a scale of one to ten how strongly would you prefer us to be using a scale of one to five?

CUSTOMER: Ten. (*Reads*) Should I have linguine for dinner?

WAITRESS: Yes, if you get on with him.

CUSTOMER: What?

WAITRESS: (*reads*) Would you prefer the water for your tea to be heated by gas, electricity or fire wood?

CUSTOMER: All three. I do like to know it's been heated through properly. (*Reads*) Should I take up yoga?

WAITRESS: Um... yes.

CUSTOMER: (*amused*) Don't you mean 'ommm... yes'?

WAITRESS: What?

CUSTOMER: Never mind.

WAITRESS: (*reads*) Do you have a preferred energy supplier?

CUSTOMER: Oh yes. Oh, hang on a minute. It'll come to me. Just hold on a minute. It will come to me. Got it. Lucozade.

WAITRESS: (*puzzled*) Lucozade?

CUSTOMER: (*reads*) Should I take a year off?

WAITRESS: If you mean off your age, then yes. (*Reads*) Would you be prepared to wait three weeks for a cup of tea while we changed our electricity supplier?

CUSTOMER: Well, that would depend on how thirsty I was.

WAITRESS: (*quietly*) Oh.

CUSTOMER: And in my last question I meant 'Should I take a year off work?' I'm an air traffic controller.

WAITRESS: In that case, no. It would be far too dangerous. (*Reads*) Would you prefer that this café was an optician's?

CUSTOMER: I thought it was. That's why I came in. (*Reads*) Should I become a Christian?

WAITRESS: Why not? To hell with the consequences. (*Reads*) Would you prefer that this café was a hairdresser's?

CUSTOMER: Yes.

WAITRESS: What? You would prefer that this café was a hairdresser's?

CUSTOMER: Yes. I think I would.

WAITRESS: (*increasingly emotional*) Oh my god. I'm going to have to go and let head office know. I loved working here. It was my dream job. And I don't know anything about hairdressing. Well that's it, isn't it? The dream is over. The dream is over.

CUSTOMER stands and walks over to WAITRESS.

CUSTOMER: Come on now. Get a grip.

CUSTOMER puts hands around WAITRESS'S shoulders to calm her. A beat. Removes hands.

CUSTOMER: Just listen to us. Here's you, an employee of a large global company, and here's me, a strong independent woman, and we have to ask complete strangers their opinions and then act on them.

WAITRESS: You're absolutely right. I mean, how daft is that? On a scale of one to ten. Oh my god, I can't stop doing it.

CUSTOMER puts hands around WAITRESS'S shoulders again.

122

CUSTOMER: Yes you can (*removes hands*). Anyway, I'm just as bad (*walks to chair and sits*). You'd think I'd be able to decide for myself whether to have yoga for dinner and if I should take up linguine.

WAITRESS: And I'm sure you can. With a bit of practice. I've certainly learnt my lesson. I won't be conducting any more surveys for a while.

CUSTOMER: I'm glad to hear it (*stands and picks up handbag to leave*). And you listen to me: your dream is not over.

WAITRESS: You mean I'm still asleep?

CUSTOMER: No, I mean your dream of working here is not over.

WAITRESS: It isn't?

CUSTOMER: No, of course not.

WAITRESS: You're absolutely right. Of course it isn't. I'll soon get the hang of this hairdressing lark, won't I? Take a seat.

WAITRESS pushes CUSTOMER down into chair and puts tea towel around CUSTOMER'S neck like a hairdressing cape.

WAITRESS: Now, let me see. How about a few highlights maybe? (*Produces scissors from apron pocket.*) Or what about an inch off the length?

CUSTOMER stands and exits hurriedly.

WAITRESS: Where are you going? Wait. Come back (*runs after CUSTOMER brandishing scissors and exits*).

THE END

Survey by Hugh Smith

The Emperor's New Clothes

by Derek Webb

Characters
DAVE – jack-the-lad type (20-50)
BRIAN – his sidekick (20-50)
LANDLADY – pub landlady

Synopsis
Two men appear to be carrying a large object (about 1 x 2 metres)
that they claim to be a work of art, but to everyone but them it is
invisible…

Setting and properties
Two chairs, two beer glasses

The Author
DEREK WEBB's 1-act and full length plays have been performed throughout the world. His series of full length murder mystery comedies *'Agatha Crusty and…'* have already notched up dozens of productions, including the USA and Australia, as well as the UK.

He has written several other full length stage plays, the latest of which was *The Railway Children Lady* about the life of children's author, Edith Nesbit. In 2013, his play *Call Me Dusty* celebrated the 50th Anniversary of the start of Dusty Springfield's career and toured to 13 venues to great success.

He has also abridged many dozens of books for Hodder Headline, Random House and Harper Collins among others. These have ranged from Jane Austen to Ruth Rendell. He has dramatised a large number of children's books for audio, including The Minpins and Esio Trot by Raold Dahl and 80 minute dramatisations of children's classics including The Secret Garden, The Railway Children and The Incredible Journey.

His novel for 9-12 year olds called *'Is'*, about a girl who believes she is Isambard Kingdom Brunel reincarnated, is published by Parthian.

As the play begins two men make their way slowly into the playing space. Each has his arms outstretched, one above the other, as if carrying a large object between them. As they make their way through the audience, DAVE, who is in the lead, calls out:

DAVE: 'Scuse me... Thanks. Sorry, could I... Thanks...

They reach the playing space.

DAVE: Let's just put it down here shall we?

They gently lift 'the object' to the ground and stand holding 'it' by its top edge.

DAVE: Get a couple of chairs will you Brian? And we can prop it up.

BRIAN: You got it?

DAVE: Yeah, sure.

BRIAN lets go of his end of the object and goes to get two chairs which he puts with their backs to 'the object'.

DAVE: Right, lets lean it up against them.

BRIAN then takes his end of 'the object' again and they gently lean it against the chair backs. They both stand back and admire 'the object'

DAVE: Well, what do you think?

BRIAN: It's difficult to know what to say. I mean I've never seen anything like it before.

DAVE: Worth a bob or two that is. It's an original Jackson Perry.

BRIAN: It's certainly original, I'll say that for it.

BRIAN gets down and peers closely at 'the object'

DAVE: I mean look at that brush work. That's a genius at work that is. You don't often see work that fine. It's – it's exquisite, that's what it is.

BRIAN: Exquisite.

DAVE: Oh yes, quite takes the breath away, doesn't it?

BRIAN: Breath away, yes.

DAVE: It's very rare you'll see something like this on the market you know.

BRIAN: No, I can see that.

DAVE: So when one comes along, you've just got to grab it.

BRIAN: If you see it.

DAVE: Like you say, if you see it.

BRIAN goes closer and gets on his knees to inspect 'the object'

BRIAN: What did you say it was called, Dave?

DAVE: 'The Emperor's New Clothes'

BRIAN: That's an unusual title.

DAVE: It's a very unusual piece.

BRIAN: It certainly is.

BRIAN gets back up.

So this bloke who sold it to you Dave. He was like an art dealer was he?

DAVE: No, to be honest Brian, I don't think he knew what he had here. He wouldn't have recognized it if it'd jumped up and bit him.

BRIAN: Yeah, but that's a bit unlikely, isn't it Dave?

DAVE: He dealt in junk mainly. The shop was just stuffed full with old rubbish. Worthless most of it.

BRIAN: But you spotted this all right!

DAVE: In this game, Brian, you've got to keep your wits about you. The minute I laid my eyes on this beauty I knew I'd found something rather special.

BRIAN: So go on, Dave, what'd you pay for it?

DAVE: Ah, that would be telling, old son.

BRIAN: Yeah that's right… Go on, tell me.

Pause.

DAVE: You can't put a price on genius, Brian.

BRIAN: You're saying it's priceless?

DAVE: Or valueless, if you prefer.

BRIAN: Worthless you mean?

DAVE: I didn't say that.

BRIAN: So how much did you pay for it?

DAVE: Let's just say that the bloke in the shop obviously couldn't see what he had there. But I've got a nose for great art, Brian. I knew what it would fetch, even if he didn't.

BRIAN: So you got it cheap did you?

DAVE: I got myself a bargain, I know that. I tell you Brian, I couldn't believe my eyes when I saw it.

BRIAN: No, I'm sure.

DAVE turns BRIAN around to face 'the object'

DAVE: Tell me honestly Brian, what does it say to you?

BRIAN: What does it say to me? I can't actually hear it say anything, Dave. I can't hear a sound. I can't even smell it either.

DAVE: Smell it? Why would you smell it?

BRIAN: You said you had a nose for art, so I thought maybe, since I couldn't see it or hear it, I might be able to smell it.

DAVE: It doesn't work like that.

BRIAN: No, I suppose you're right. So how exactly am I going to be able to recognise great art when I see it – or rather don't see it?

DAVE: It's a skill like everything else, Brian. You can develop it. It's taken me quite a while, you know. I mean – you may find this difficult to believe – but I didn't used to be this tuned into art. I thought a lot of modern art was just like someone splashing paint around. I really couldn't see the point of it.

BRIAN: It's what they used to call abstract, isn't it?

DAVE points at 'the object'

DAVE: *This* is abstract, Brian. You don't get much more abstract than this.

BRIAN: No, that's true.

DAVE: Look at the sheer purity of it. I mean you may say there's nothing to it, but let me tell you that to create something of this simplicity takes real talent, real genius. Doesn't it just take your breath away?

BRIAN: Well... But...

DAVE: Yes? Come on, out with it, you've got something you want to say haven't you?

BRIAN: Well, yes, it's just that...

DAVE: Yes?

BRIAN: The thing is... And I know it's like pure genius and all that... But...

DAVE: Come on, spit it out.

BRIAN: It just occurs to me that, well, it's very simple in its own way, isn't it?

DAVE: Simple?

BRIAN: Yeah, like clean...

DAVE: Clean – uncluttered you mean?

BRIAN: Yeah, sort of simplistic.

DAVE: That's the genius of Jackson Perry, that is Brian. The man is an absolute master of simplicity. He reduces complex concepts down to their basics. He distils thoughts and ideas – clearing everything out of the way, until he gets to the pure essence of life.

BRIAN: Well, that's my point really.

DAVE: What's your point, Brian?

BRIAN: It's like he's had an idea here with this 'Emperor's New Clothes' painting and he's sort of reduced it down to something which is – well – pure like you say, so pure it's kind of transparent.

DAVE: Transparently obvious, is that what you're saying?

BRIAN: It's certainly transparent.

DAVE: He is a genius isn't he?

BRIAN: No doubt, Dave, but on the other hand, there's not a lot to it is there?

DAVE: That's rather the point isn't it? It allows the viewer to inject their personality into it.

BRIAN: I don't quite see that.

DAVE: No, you don't get it, do you Brian?

BRIAN: Oh, I think I do. The thing is, being as it's so pure, so clean, so distilled as you say... well there's not a lot left is there? Nothing in fact.

DAVE: Yes, that's the beauty of it.

BRIAN: But being as there's not a lot to it, so to speak. Well sod all really...

DAVE: Where is this going, Brian?

BRIAN: I was just thinking... it would be really very easy to...

DAVE: Yes?

BRIAN: To forge it, wouldn't it?

There's a stunned silence

DAVE: *Forge* it?

BRIAN: Well, yes. I mean it wouldn't be difficult. I could do it even.

DAVE: You! You could forge a genuine Jackson Perry?

BRIAN: One like this – yes, I think so. Shall I show you?

DAVE: That won't be necessary Brian. But – well – I am a little surprised by your – how shall I say this? – Your – hubris...

BRIAN: What's that mean?

DAVE: Does it matter? *(Beat)* I have to say Dave, that I am more than a little disappointed... It's not like you...

BRIAN: I'm sorry, it just seems so obvious – forging it would be an absolute doddle. Nothing to it really – literally.

DAVE tries to maintain a straight face but fails and bursts out laughing.

BRIAN: What's so funny?

DAVE: Oh, you've rumbled me old son.

BRIAN: What d'you mean?

DAVE: This isn't the original!

BRIAN: It isn't?

DAVE: No I flogged that weeks ago.

BRIAN: So what's this?

DAVE: it's what you said – a forgery!

BRIAN goes over and inspects it carefully again.

BRIAN: I'd never have guessed. Really, Dave, you are pretty good.

DAVE: Thank you.

BRIAN: So what did you do with the original?

DAVE: Flogged it – to a bloke down the pub

BRIAN: Did you get much for it?

DAVE: Not really. But it was worth a couple of pints.

BRIAN: That's not so good.

DAVE: I did the same with the first forgery a few days later. And another six of them.

BRIAN: What! So you can just keep selling it? Over and over?

DAVE: Exactly!

BRIAN: Now that is genius, Dave!

DAVE has a very smug expression.

DAVE: I've already sold this one as it happens.

BRIAN: Really? Who to?

DAVE: The pub landlady.

BRIAN: Great!

DAVE: Here she comes now.

The pub LANDLADY appears carrying two pint glasses.

LANDLADY: Here we are, gentlemen, two pints of best!

She hands them a glass each. Both are completely empty. They each look at their glass and then at each other in astonishment.

THE END

The Emperor's New Clothes by Derek Webb

Casabangor

by Peter Hurd

Characters
HARRY SNELL – Bogey
DR TAYLOR – a psychiatrist
SAMANTHA – a waitress

Synopsis
An escapee from the local psychiatric unit, who believes he is the on-screen persona of Humphrey Bogart, is ruminating on the 'death' of his partner.

Setting & Properties
A coffee shop in Bangor, North wales, on a rainy day. A table and two chairs. Cigarettes, lighter and cups. Mobile phone and umbrella.

The Author
I live in N. Wales with my wife and cat and this is my first success at scriptwriting. This play was inspired by the graphic novel "The Bogie Man" By John Wagner, Alan Grant and Robin Smith and is a tribute to their work. Two creative writing groups – Riverside Writers and Bangor Cellar Writers – have been instrumental in giving me the confidence to forge on as a writer and I thank them for their support.

HARRY in a trilby and raincoat sits at a table. An empty chair is next to him. He sips from a cup of coffee and grimaces. On the table is a packet of cigarettes and a zippo lighter. He puts the cup of coffee down and licks lips.

HARRY: It was raining again. I'd only been here a week but already I was beginning to forget what the sun looked like and how a good cup of joe' should taste. Bangor, Wales. The place had been billed as the cultural epicentre of the North but so far all I'd experienced was bad coffee and the beginnings of a cold. Not that I was here for culture anyways. I was following up a case that my partner Marlowe had been close to finishing. Poor Marlowe. He'd washed up on the shores of the Menai Straits near a place called 'Bow-Maries' with a bullet hole in his head the size of a grapefruit. The local cops ruled out suicide and began an investigation that led to no-wheresville. Amateurs. Me and Marlowe had been living and breathing 'investigations' for twenny years as private investigators. Now I was left to pick up the pieces, finish the case and avenge my partner's death.

Pause.

He'd took a job for a dame name of Trixie LaBouche; cute name for a cute doll. Marlowe was always a sucker for a pretty face and a bust you could hang a cuppa coffee on. Seemed her ex-partner owed her some dough… a lotta dough and had done a moonlight flit across the pond. The last I'd heard from Marlowe was that he was close, real close to tracking him down and putting the squeeze on him. He'd been staking out a two bit joint called 'The Blue Sky Café' hoping to collar her ex-partner with a view to pumping him for information. Marlowe had no name to go by. Only the moniker of 'the fat man'. Not a lot to hang on but this fat man had a birth mark the shape of a moose's head on his left shoulder. According to the local boys in blue he'd been accosting too many fat men about taking off their shirts. Looks like they coulda been right. Or maybe…just maybe he got too close to the truth. Either way it was up to me to put a lid on it.

Enter stage left WAITRESS. She has a name tag with the name Samantha written on it.

WAITRESS: Would you like another coffee?

HARRY: Sure sweetheart…and this time put some beans in it will ya?

WAITRESS pulls a face and exits.

HARRY: The waitress gave me a look like a Rabbi forced ta eat a bacon sandwich and then went back around the corner. She was cute: another time, another place we coulda made the earth move but I was on a case.

Looks disdainfully at coffee cup left on table, picks it up.

No refills.

Places cup back down.

I sure was running up a tab on coffee but, seeing as LaBouche was paying my expenses, what did I care?

DR TAYLOR appears stage right shaking down an umbrella looking across stage as if searching for someone.

HARRY: Then, as if just by thinking of her, she appeared at the doorway shaking down an umbrella. In all the cafés in all of Bangor she had ta walk inta mine. Marlowe's femme-fatale...Trixie Labouche.

DR TAYLOR walks over to the table.

HARRY: She strode over to my table like she was walking on air,

She sits down.

pulled up a seat and sat down, the smell of her perfume stinging my eyes like mace.

DR TAYLOR: Harry, who are you talking to?

HARRY: *(to audience)* I'd only seen pictures of her before in swanky magazines on the rich and famous. They truly didn't do her justice.

(Looks at DR TAYLOR.) Hey beautiful, long time no see, what's up?

DR TAYLOR: Look Harry, I don't know how you got out but we've been looking everywhere for you. You're not a well man! Please come back to the institution with me, eh? We can jump in my car and be back in Llanfairfechan in time for tea. What do you say?

HARRY: *(looking at audience)* Clan ferwhat? Her voice was as rich as cream and molasses but what she was saying just curdled the cream.

DR TAYLOR: Oh dear, you've got worse haven't you poor love.

HARRY: *(to DR TAYLOR)* Look doll face, quit playing games. Don't worry about a thing. I'm close, real close. You'll get your money.

DR TAYLOR: Money? What Money? Look, Mr. Snell, you're having a relapse. Come back to the institution with me and we'll sort everything out. It's roly-poly for pudding and Dr Who on the telly. You like him don't you?

HARRY: *(to audience)* Dr Who? What was she playing at? I stared at her long and hard. *(Stares at DR TAYLOR.)*

DR TAYLOR: Harry? Hello? *(Waves hand in front of his face. No reaction from HARRY.)*

HARRY: *(to audience)* Something stank, real bad, worse than the trash cans outside my local deli on the corner of 5th and Brooklyn Avenue back home.

DR TAYLOR: *(takes phone out of pocket)* I'd better ring and tell them you're OK. Alright? *(Shakes head.)*

HARRY: *(to audience)* Maybe the fat man had got to her, struck up a deal. Whatever it was it was starting to make me feel uncomfortable.

DR TAYLOR: *(into phone)* Oh hi Geoff. Yeah… I'm sitting with him now.

HARRY: *(to audience)* The hairs on the back of my neck started to itch. I hadn't had that feeling since my gun running days off the coast of Algiers.

DR TAYLOR: Yeah… now he's talking into space… I know… mad as a hatter… hang on a mo. I'll call you back. *(Puts phone away.)*

HARRY: *(to DR TAYLOR)* Listen sweetheart, whatever game you're playing it ain't gonna work. No one plays me for a patsy.

DR TAYLOR: A what?

HARRY: *(to DR TAYLOR)* A patsy, a patsy! Marlowe's dead and I aim ta get the punk who laid him on ice, with or without your help. Get in my way and you'll regret it… maybe not today, maybe not tomorrow but soon and for the rest of your life.

DR TAYLOR: OK, OK. Calm down. Let's not do anything too hasty, eh?

HARRY: *(to audience)* She stared so hard at me that I could almost hear her brain ticking over. *(Takes a cigarette out of the packet and lights up.)* I lit a cigarette and let the smoke mist over her eyes.

DR TAYLOR coughs and waves the smoke away.

HARRY: *(to audience)* She coughed like a rich dame should do.

DR TAYLOR: Harry, it's non-smoking in here you really should…

HARRY puts out the cigarette in the coffee cup.

HARRY: *(to DR TAYLOR)* What's with calling me 'Harry' toots? Ya forgotten the name of the guy ya hired? Let me make it simple for ya. Bogey, just call me Bogey.

DR TAYLOR sighs, rubs temple with left hand and stares at HARRY

DR TAYLOR: Oh… dear.

HARRY: *(to audience)* She sighed real hard and rubbed her forehead with her left hand then give me a look the sphinx woulda been proud of.

DR TAYLOR: Your name is Harry Snell and you run a carpet warehouse off the A55 near Prestatyn. You were admitted into my care in March after your twin brother, Marion died in a car crash on the M62 whilst on a business trip to Hull. My name is Dr Taylor. *(Puts a hand on his sleeve.)* Please try to remember.

Pause.

HARRY: *(to audience)* She laid a hand on my sleeve and gave me that Bambi in the woods look that had helped make her famous. Hell, I didn't know what she was playing at but I knew for sure that this wasn't right.

DR TAYLOR: Think Harry, think! It was only last week we went on a day trip to Chester and met that family from Bavaria at the European market outside the tourist information centre.

HARRY: *(to DR TAYLOR, nodding)* I remember it well. You wore white and the Germans wore grey. But it was Paris sweetheart, just before the city fell... the last time we were together.

(To audience) The war had only just begun and life in the city of love was good. I knew she adored me, hell needed me, but only because she thought her husband was dead...

DR TAYLOR: Harry, Harry... I'm single, remember...

HARRY: *(to audience)*...and maybe I loved her too.

DR TAYLOR: ...and gay.

Suddenly HARRY grabs both her hands.

HARRY: *(to DR TAYLOR)* Sure we were happy but for how long would that a' lasted? He needs you and the resistance need him to continue his work. Without your love and support...

DR TAYLOR: Oooh, haven't you got a firm grip! A little too firm actually...

HARRY lets go of her hands.

HARRY: *(to DR TAYLOR)* Go to him, get out of here! I don't love you! I never have!

WAITRESS enters stage left holding a cup of coffee.

WAITRESS: Is everything alright?

DR TAYLOR: Oh yes, thankyou. We're going in a minute.

WAITRESS: OK then. *(Places cup down on table.)* If you need anything just ask for Sam.

HARRY: *(to WAITRESS)* God bless ya Sam. *(Looks her up and down.)* Boy have you been through a few changes.

WAITRESS: I beg your pardon?

DR TAYLOR: There's no need to be rude Harry! *(To WAITRESS)* He's having a bit of an off day.

WAITRESS: Right... *(Exits)*

HARRY: *(after WAITRESS)* When ya get ta the piano you know what I want ta hear. You played it for her, now play it for me!

DR TAYLOR: Now Harry, don't cause a scene.

HARRY: *(after WAITRESS)* Play it again Sam!

DR TAYLOR: Stop it this instant Harry, look at me...I need you to finish...

HARRY: *(turns his head back to audience.)* It was Trixie again. Did she never give up? Didn't she understand?

DR TAYLOR: Why on earth do you keep doing that 'talking into nowhere' thing? *(Waves hand in front of his face. Again, no reaction.)*

HARRY: *(to audience)* Hell, I coulda given up, I coulda got the first plane back to the states but in my line of work if you don't get even for your partner getting greased then your name ain't worth a dime.

(To DR TAYLOR) Listen sugar lips, you know I'm good for it so the only other reason you could be here is to try and get back into my pocket book, and that ain't gonna happen. Unnerstand?

DR TAYLOR: I really don't know where you're going with this...

HARRY: *(to DR TAYLOR)* Going? Why sure. Hell we can't stay here! The krauts'll be all over us by the time we've had the chance ta sing the first few bars of the *Marseillaise*.

DR TAYLOR: The Marseillaise?

HARRY: *(to DR TAYLOR)* Enough small talk. *(Stands up.)* We've got a plane to catch.

DR TAYLOR: *(stands up.)* OK...maybe we could get to the plane in my car.

HARRY: *(to audience)* For a well-to-do broad she could still be spot on the money and break a few hearts at the same time.

(To DR TAYLOR) You know, this could be the start of a beautiful friendship.

138

DR TAYLOR: *(taking Harry's arm)* Indeed Har...Bogey. Indeed.

THE END

Casabangor by Peter Hurd

A Night to Remember

by Andrew Turner

© Andrew Turner 2016

Characters
CAROL – Wife
NIGEL – Husband
MARK – Police Officer

Synopsis
A middle-aged couple hope a little role play might spice up their marriage.

Setting
A local high street in the early evening

Author
ANDREW TURNER is a writer and Social Worker from Bolton. He has written several stage plays which have been performed across the United Kingdom by a number of theatre companies. Many of his short plays have been featured in the annual Arundel Festival and he has also had his work performed live on local radio. This is Andrew's first Pint-Sized Play and he is delighted and very proud that it won the Best Script Runner up 2016.

NIGEL, late forties, dressed in a cheap suit. He looks furtive and a bit shifty. NIGEL approaches CAROL, similar age. CAROL is leaning against a wall, dressed in a large light coloured overcoat and very high heels. She has her arms folded and has clearly got the hump.

NIGEL: (*in a passable American accent*) Excuse me, I'm er, I'm looking for Beverley Hills.

CAROL: Beverley Hills? I'll give you Beverly Hills in a minute. Forty friggin' minutes I've been stood here freezing my tits off.

NIGEL drops the accent.

NIGEL: I ran into Phil Ginty on the High Street. You know what he's like, I couldn't get away. Wanted to know why I was all suited and booted, this time of night.

CAROL: (*mortified*) Please tell me you didn't say what we're/

NIGEL: 'Course I didn't, what d'you take me for?

CAROL: My god if this got out I'd never show my face (*Suddenly realising*) Hold on, why aren't you in the car?

NIGEL: Well, funny thing that…apparently this area's all pedestrianised now. There's bollards up.

CAROL: You're talking bollards. Well some bloody Valentine's night this is turning out to be. D'you know where Yvonne's husband's taken her tonight?

NIGEL shakes his head.

CAROL: Maison San Jacques. Three courses, half a bottle of cava and as many Ferrero Rocher as you can jam in your handbag. Lucky cow. Even Fat Alice from Finance has been taken out, and her husband's epileptic. Well, that's it, finito, I'm going home.

NIGEL: Oh come on love. We've both got dressed up now.

CAROL thinks for a second, arms folded, scowling face.

NIGEL: (*pleadingly*) Please.

CAROL: Fine! One more go and that's it.

NIGEL: Right. You go and stand against that wall and I'll pretend I'm in the car and pull up.

CAROL huffs dramatically and slouches towards the wall again. NIGEL impersonates driving and makes the same car sound as a five year old in the playground.

CAROL: Get on with it you pillock.

NIGEL: Excuse me, I'm looking for Beverley Hills.

CAROL struts, almost tripping up, takes off her coat to reveal a very short, ill fitting dress. CAROL tries to do an American accent but it comes out Australian.

CAROL: Hey there baby, you looking for company?

NIGEL: What you talking like that for?

CAROL: I'm doing the accent.

NIGEL: Julia Roberts is American.

CAROL: I know, that's what I'm doing.

NIGEL: You sound Australian.

CAROL: No I don't. 'Hey baby', oh you're right I do. Well can I not do it in Australian then?

NIGEL: No, it's too distracting.

CAROL: Just pretend I'm Nicole Kidman...or Dame Edna!

NIGEL: No! If we're going to do it, we're going to do it right.

CAROL: Well you best hurry up or I'm putting my coat back on 'fore I catch my sodding death.

CAROL repeats 'Hey Baby' in a number of bad accents, each one nothing close to resembling an American accent.

CAROL: What about that?

NIGEL: Sounds Australian with a bit of Jamaican thrown in.

CAROL: Well I'm trying my best Nigel! I never said I was Meryl Friggin' Streep!

NIGEL: There's no need to lose your temper. You've got to, what did that therapist say: 'maintain an open dialogue throughout the exercise'.

CAROL: Piss off. And I don't know why I have to stand on a street corner dressed like a slutty lollipop lady. When he suggested role play, I don't think he meant we had to be so... literal.

NIGEL: Well we don't have to do Pretty Woman. We could do Basic Instinct if you like.

CAROL: Christ no I'm way too old to go what d'you call it... Jumanji.

NIGEL: Commando you dozy mare.

CAROL: Well that.

NIGEL: What about 9 and a half weeks?

CAROL: (*outraged*) The day before my Slimming World weigh in, I don't think so.

NIGEL sighs in exasperation.

NIGEL: Well the only other one I can think of is Fifty Shades of/

CAROL holds her hand out to stop him.

CAROL: I am not being fisted for anyone Nigel Ramsgreave so get that idea out of your head. No, we'll stick with the original plan. Right, go over there and we'll go again. The sooner we're done the better, these shoes are killing me.

NIGEL goes a short distance away and prepares himself. Slightly further away, MARK, a young man in his early twenties watches NIGEL and CAROL intently.

NIGEL: Hey baby, know how I get to Beverly Hill?

CAROL: *(in an over the top Southern American accent)* I sure do, for five dollars.

NIGEL: Five dollars!

CAROL: Just went up to ten.

NIGEL: You can't make me pay you for directions.

CAROL: I can do what I want baby, I ain't lost.

NIGEL: Fine, can you split a twenty?

CAROL takes the cash out of NIGEL's hand and sidles up to him.

CAROL: For twenty dollars I'll/

MARK suddenly leaps into action, shoving NIGEL face first against the wall and trying to cuff him.

MARK: Excuse me sir I'm arresting you under section 53a of the Sexual Offences Act 2003

NIGEL: Eh, what the hell d'you think you're playing at?

MARK: You do not have to say anything but/

CAROL: /Get off him you, that's his best suit that is. What d'you think you're doing?

MARK: What does it look like? I'm placing him under arrest.

CAROL: Arrest? What the 'eck for?

MARK: For making payment for the sexual services of a prostitute.

CAROL gasps in shock.

CAROL: Oh Nigel how could you? When were this officer?

NIGEL: He means you, you dozy bitch.

CAROL: Me! A prostitute? And what the hell gives you that idea eh?

MARK's tone becomes softer, more sympathetic.

MARK: Listen love, it's alright, you're safe now. I'll radio for back-up and we can have you off the streets and into a rehab unit within the hour.

NIGEL: You're hurting my arm.

MARK: Good. Bastards like you make me sick, preying on women for your own twisted perversions. She's a person you know, not just a prostitute.

NIGEL: She's not a prostitute!

MARK: Oh so that's your excuse is it? *(Whiney voice)* 'I didn't know she was a prostitute officer, I was just asking for directions'.

NIGEL: I was!

MARK: Look at her. The pallid, lifeless complexion, the deadness behind the eyes, the ravaged carcass of a body, destroyed by years of substance abuse and sexual degradation. It's bleeding obvious what she is.

CAROL pulls her coat around her to hide her body.

CAROL: (*hurt and self conscious*) I do Bums 'n' Tums twice a week at the Methodist Hall.

MARK talks into his radio.

MARK: I need back up at the corner of Brunswick St, picked up a kerb crawler and street walker.

NIGEL: For god's sake Carol, do something.

CAROL: Officer please there's been a massive misunderstanding here if you'll just/

CAROL puts her hand in her handbag whilst MARK tried to subdue NIGEL against the wall and direct CAROL.

MARK: Whoa, hands where I can see them now!

CAROL: I just want to/

MARK: /Hands where I can see them I said. You could be concealing a deadly weapon in that handbag.

CAROL: Not unless I intend to kill you with two Tena Lady pads and a Vagisil. Here, have a look at them.

CAROL goes over and shows MARK the photos inside her purse.

MARK: What is that, what're you showing me?

CAROL is proud of her pictures and MARK nods, interested, with the odd 'nice' comment.

CAROL: Well, that's me and our Tracey at Fountains Abbey, she had a breast off shortly after that were taken. That's me and our Bryony at my niece's naming ceremony.

MARK: Is a naming ceremony not the same as a Christening?

CAROL: Well I thought that but apparently not, a Christening has a religious element.

NIGEL: He's hurting my neck here Carol!

CAROL: Oh, yes… and that is me and my husband Nigel on the beach at Cromer.

MARK: (*realising*) Ahhh.

CAROL: So you see officer, unfortunately for me, he is my husband.

MARK thinks for a moment then releases NIGEL, who rubs his wrists like a wimp.

MARK: Fine, but would you like to tell me just what the hell a middle aged couple are doing hanging around the town centre at this time of night?

NIGEL: Tell him Carol.

CAROL: Oh no, this was your idea.

NIGEL looks sheepish and embarrassed.

NIGEL: We er, we've been seeing an advice type, counsellor sort of, sex therapist kind of person sort of thing.

MARK: (*embarrassed*) Oh.

CAROL: (*clarifying*) Things have become a bit, you know in the old bedroom department, what's the word…

MARK: Pedestrian?

CAROL: No.

MARK: Stagnant?

CAROL: No… Flaccid.

MARK: (*even more embarrassed*) Oh.

NIGEL: And this counsellor type individual thought a bit of er…role play could er…

CAROL: Could get him going again in the underwear region. You know, get a tent pitched on his conjugal campsite.

MARK: I get it. But why this kerb crawler street hooker thing?

CAROL: Ask him, it were all his idea.

NIGEL: Well it's Pretty Woman, innit? The film I mean.

MARK: Never seen it.

NIGEL: Well it was the film I took Carol to see on our first date so I thought… you know, good memories and that.

MARK: Ahhh, that's, that's quite romantic really isn't it? You're a lucky woman madam, most men can't remember where they took their wives for their last date, never mind their first.

CAROL broods for a moment.

CAROL: Lucky am I? Lucky? I saw Pretty Woman with my sister Yvonne, Nigel, so I don't know which dirty little scrubber you took, but it certainly wasn't me!

NIGEL: No we went to the cinema and then I parked round the back of The Albion and you let me…(*realising*) Oh.

CAROL: I think you'd better arrest me officer.

MARK: Arrest you? Why what for?

CAROL: 'Cos I'm about to murder my bloody husband. Get here you bastard!

NIGEL runs off, hotly pursued by CAROL with MARK following on, calling for backup.

THE END

A Night to Remember by Andrew Turner